Village of

NORTH PALM BEACH

Village of NORTH PALM BEACH

• A HISTORY •

ROSA SOPHIA

Foreword by Mayor Darryl Aubrey

Published by The History Press
Charleston, SC
www.historypress.com

Cover image of the Village of North Palm Beach, used with permission.

First published 2020

Manufactured in the United States

ISBN 9781467143110

Library of Congress Control Number: 2019956042

Notice: The information in this book is true and complete to the best of our knowledge. It is offered without guarantee on the part of the author or The History Press. The author and The History Press disclaim all liability in connection with the use of this book.

This book is dedicated to North Palm Beach Village Clerk Melissa Teal (1958–2019).

It is also dedicated to Heavy Head, whose friendship I will always treasure (1935–2018).

And, finally, this book is dedicated to all those who built the Village of North Palm Beach into the community it is today.

CONTENTS

A SPECIAL TRIBUTE

Melissa Teal is one of the people to whom I dedicated this book. Because of her contributions, she also deserves a special tribute here. She served North Palm Beach as the village clerk for thirty years, and she was always available to answer questions and assist me. On July 19, 2019, Melissa suddenly passed away. Just a few weeks before, we had been corresponding via email. She helped me acquire many of the photos that you will find in this book.

When I recorded oral history interviews with North Palm Beach residents in the village hall, she made sure that we had a quiet meeting room to use. When I started digitizing the archives and making them available to residents online, Melissa provided valuable support. As the village clerk, she had a never-ending list of duties to attend to, but she always made time to answer my questions and assist me to the best of her ability. When I left the position, Lynn Holden—my mother—took over as the village historian. Melissa always took time out of her busy schedule to help my mother whenever she had difficulties in scanning and digitizing archival materials.

Melissa was not only a tremendous support to me when I served as the village historian, but she also continued to help me after I left the position. I was still researching and writing about North Palm Beach's history, and Melissa was always there. I am eternally grateful for her continuous support of my mission to preserve village history. She will be greatly missed.

To learn more about the village and to look through the village's online archives, please visit: *www.village-npb.org/221/Village-Historian.*

F L O R I D A

If you have longed to really live in the heart of Florida's fabulous Gold Coast . . . with your own boat right at your doorstep . . . for a private Golf and Country Club complete with tennis courts and an Olympic size pool . . . fishing from your own front lawn, or the more exciting sport of deep sea or Gulf Stream fishing within a few minutes from your home . . . stop dreaming and enjoy it . . . the Village of North Palm Beach was created with you in mind.

The Village of North Palm Beach is located on the sunny shores of Lake Worth, just 3 miles north of Palm Beach. Over 1200 acres of the estate of the late Sir Harry Oakes is the setting for this perfect tropical community. Of the 3500 spacious homesites, over one half are situated on the miles of cool waterways that interlace the property.

The Village of North Palm Beach will be entirely self-contained with its own Shopping Plaza, Country Club, Marina and Yacht Club . . . schools, churches, parks and recreational centers . . . its own water plant, sewage and garbage disposal system, private streets and miles of waterways. The Village of North Palm Beach reflects Florida Living at its best.

This advertisement was published in the 1956 *Parade of Homes Plan Book*, which was sponsored by the Home Builders Association of Palm Beach County. *Village of North Palm Beach.*

FOREWORD

The Village of North Palm Beach is a community of about thirteen thousand year-round residents, and it swells to about twenty thousand during the winter season. North Palm Beach occupies some 5.8 square miles that include canals, bodies of water, parks, recreational facilities, an outstanding library and residential neighborhoods with houses that range from middle-income homes to multi-million-dollar waterfront mansions. Many of North Palm Beach's residents love boating and enjoy the village's 2.2 square miles of water, which include many miles of canals. The village is also home to a Jack Nicklaus signature golf course, one of only two such municipal golf courses in the United States. And as these words are being written, the construction of a magnificent new clubhouse is nearing completion. As a center for golf, dining, swimming and tennis, the new clubhouse will be a family-oriented gathering place.

North Palm Beach has an interesting history that is often overlooked when it is compared to those of the larger communities around it. This book was written by Rosa Sophia, who served as the village historian of North Palm Beach from December 9, 2010, to March 27, 2014. This book brings the history of North Palm Beach to life, starting with the pre-history of the area and ending with events of the present day. Many eccentric and notable people have played key roles in the village's history, and this book brings them back to life for the reader. These individuals include Dr. Munyon, who built a health retreat on what is now Munyon Island; Harry Kelsey; Sir Harry Oakes; and John D. MacArthur, whose Foundation donated the land for John D. MacArthur Beach State Park. There are many other colorful characters whom you will learn about in this book.

It has been a highlight in my life to serve on the village council for the past fourteen years, including the four terms I served as the village mayor. Today, North Palm Beach is best described by its motto. It truly is "the best place to live under the sun."

—Dr. Darryl Aubrey,
mayor of North Palm Beach, Florida

PREFACE

The year was 2010 when I took a job as a clerk at the North Palm Beach Public Library. At this time, I also began studying Florida history. I had no idea I was about to embark on a journey that would lead me to write this book. One day, our reference librarian mentioned that the volunteer position of village historian—a council-appointed job—might be available, and she suggested that I apply. Although I grappled with feelings of being under-qualified, I did have a few ideas for revitalizing the history archives. Once I'd given it some thought, I turned in an application and was called to a Tuesday evening council meeting. At the podium, I recited a speech that I had practiced, listing and explaining my ideas for rejuvenating the history office. I told the council that I felt it was important to digitize the archives so residents could easily look up historical information via the village's website. I also mentioned that the history office could raise awareness of the village's history through community outreach and a newsletter that would be distributed at the library. Afterward, the council voted, and I was appointed to the position of village historian.

I walked into the office—the village history archives—not knowing where to begin. I networked with other historians and archivists in the area and asked them for their advice. I later joined the Society of Florida Archivists and the Gold Coast Archivists. I also asked for help from the Historical Society of Palm Beach County. Once I consulted a number of helpful sources, I started digitizing the village's archives to the best of my ability. But most of all, I studied, learned and listened while serving in this position. I also regularly wrote a history newsletter, which I printed and distributed at the library, and I started a companion blog. Whenever I got a detail wrong, I received a pleasant phone call from a resident who was eager to share their information. Every mistake I made taught me something new and opened new doors. I have endeavored to make this book as comprehensive as possible. History is fluid, and we're always learning new things. I suspect that I will learn things later that I wish I could have included here—there will always be more to share and more to absorb.

While writing this history of North Palm Beach, specifically, I also shared pertinent information regarding the relationship between North Palm Beach and surrounding towns. It is impossible to discuss the village without also discussing how the village has been shaped by what is now Lake Park, Palm Beach Gardens and Juno Beach. I also relied on archives that came from outside the village, including those maintained by the Lake Park Historical Society and the Historical Society of Palm Beach County.

All of the people I interviewed became the inspirations for this book. I heard the stories of those who moved to the village to build better lives for their families. Those individuals have contributed to the history of North Palm Beach, whether their contributions were large or small.

I hope this book helps to preserve and honor the memories and contributions of all those who have called North Palm Beach home.

ACKNOWLEDGEMENTS

I must thank everyone who assisted me while I researched and wrote this book, including everyone who was kind enough to speak with me on the phone and answer my questions in person. Some of these individuals have been quoted in the book, while others offered valuable insight that helped me better understand North Palm Beach's beginnings and the people who made it what it is today.

Thank you to the Huls family, Pam Thomas Wagner, Andrew Foster, Dr. Darryl Aubrey, Jane Higginbotham, Joanna Hogan, Lucky Arnold, John Bills, Ann Swiatowski, Ray Eberling, Christine Schwencke Sams, Christine DelGuzzi, Steve Higgins, Jeanne Saunders, Susan Tiedemann Bickel, Joe J. Eassa, Margaret Robson, Richard Cavanah, Michelle Wentling, Linda Paraizo, Wendell McEver, Jane Sanders, Judy Pierman, Joseph A. Tringali, Charlotte Young Doten, Claire Hill, Robin Murphy and Nancy Fant Moore.

I would also like to thank the Village of North Palm Beach and, most of all, village clerk Melissa Teal. I also want to give thanks to Lynn Ruiz and the staff of the North Palm Beach Public Library—past and present—and the many friends I've made at the library along the way. I want to give many thanks to Debi Murray of the Historical Society of Palm Beach County; L.J. Parker of the Lake Park Historical Society; Josh Liller, historian and collections manager at the Jupiter Inlet Lighthouse and Museum and co-author of the revised edition of *Five Thousand Years on the Loxahatchee: A Pictorial History of Jupiter-Tequesta, Florida*; Janet DeVries, author and co-author of numerous books, including *Overdue in Paradise: The*

Library History of Palm Beach County (Palmango Press); Ruth Berge, author of *Growing Up in Northern Palm Beach County* (The History Press); John and Mary Lou Missall, authors of *The Army Is My Calling: The Life and Writings of Major John Rogers Vinton* (Florida Historical Society Press); Ruby Lynn Holden, village historian of North Palm Beach from 2014 to 2016; Scott Edwards of the Bureau of Historic Preservation and the Florida Historic Golf Trail; and the Tallahassee Historical Society.

I must also extend my appreciation to all of my friends in history, along with my friends, teachers and mentors in the writing world. They all continue to encourage and support me, especially my dear friend Richard Procyk and my colleagues at the Seminole Wars Foundation and the Loxahatchee Battlefield Preservationists. Finally, I want to give a warm thank-you to Carolyn Smith, Stephanie Piccino and all of my friends at the Palm City Library and Martin County Library System for putting up with my constant history chatter and random anecdotes about North Palm Beach—I love you all! Last, but not least, I want to say thank you to The History Press and my editor, Joe Gartrell, for believing in this project.

INTRODUCTION

The Village of North Palm Beach's history is not very visible on the surface. The village's old Winter Club was once a landmark that people would name when referencing the area, but it was demolished in 1984, despite some residents' efforts to save it. North Palm Beach's more subtle structures, like the village hall (designed by architect John L. Volk) and local churches, and Winship's Prescription Center—its longest-running business—remain the only physical nods to the village's past. However, it is the community's time-tested atmosphere that truly defines North Palm Beach.

While the village is still relatively young, there has been a lot of change in the surrounding area over many centuries. Those who lived in the village during its early years remember when Northlake Boulevard was just a dirt road west of Military Trail; sandy scrub still stretched across the landscape. In 1963, only a few years after the village's incorporation, Northlake was a two-lane road with only two stop signs—one at Prosperity Farms Road and one at U.S. Highway 1. People who grew up in North Palm Beach can think back and remember a carefree childhood. Kids rode their bicycles to the beach, and families went boating around this water-centered community; there were clubs, social activities and get-togethers, and of course, golf was a big part of the village.

When North Palm Beach reached sixty years of age, it seemed right for the village to have a chronology of its own history. Within this history are the lives of those who traveled to South Florida. They all came for different

The Village of North Palm Beach was the first community in Florida to be given the National Award of Merit from the National Association of Home Builders, as advertised in this 1956 brochure. *Village of North Palm Beach.*

reasons, but they all shared a common focus: They were following a dream, and many of them were trying to build prosperous lives for their families.

The nearby town of Lake Park, formerly Kelsey City, was the product of Harry Kelsey's dream of building an idyllic community where all of life's necessities are within reach. Later on, much of the land in Lake Park was purchased by John D. MacArthur, and when North Palm Beach was incorporated, a loophole kept it as a part of Lake Park for several years. Other figures in North Palm Beach's early history include a number of developers, like the Ross brothers (known by many as Bob and Dick), Jack Schwencke and Jay H. White; library society members and librarians, like Nancy Fant Moore; village manager Albin Olson; and art center director Ed Jacomo. These people, and many more, made up the fabric of a community that began as a village spurred on by local economic growth. Many new residents were drawn to the area by the Pratt & Whitney facility constructed on the west side of town, off the Beeline Highway, in 1956. RCA—the Radio Corporation of America—arrived in Palm Beach Gardens in 1960, and they both contributed

Construction of homes in 1959. *Village of North Palm Beach.*

to local economic growth. While Pratt & Whitney employees moved to South Florida to follow a career, others chose to move to North Palm Beach, which had been planned with professionals and young families in mind.

Although 1956 is considered recent history, the seeds of a village were planted long before North Palm Beach was incorporated. The village was built during a memorable and impactful time in American history—a time which shaped the future of the country. In 1956, Dwight D. Eisenhower was the president of the United States, and Elvis Presley had just made his first appearance on *The Ed Sullivan Show*. It was a time of great change for the country, and it was a turning point for South Florida, as more and more people flocked to the Sunshine State.

Due to careful planning and strategy, the Ross brothers, Jay H. White and Jack Schwencke were able to create a village that, to this day, retains what many residents feel is a small-town community atmosphere. Because of this planning, North Palm Beach became the first settlement in Florida to receive the National Association of Home Builders' award for excellence in 1958.

THE BEST PLACE TO LIVE UNDER THE SUN

North Palm Beach's motto captures the essence of the village. It is "the best place to live under the sun." It has three small parks—Anchorage Park, Lakeside Park and Osborne Park—as well as a community pool, country club, community center and library. It also has MacArthur Beach State Park, which features two miles of pristine beach, nature trails and a glimpse into Florida's past. In 1960, the population of North Palm Beach was a mere 2,684.

In the spring of 1973, the University of North Carolina compiled a community profile of North Palm Beach and released the findings in July 1974. In making the profile, the university interviewed 202 North Palm Beach residents. Their findings were compared with the "less planned" control community of Tequesta, Florida, as well as thirteen other newly incorporated communities around the country.

In 1973, 99.4 percent of the village's respondents to the university's survey were white. Just over 44 percent were fifty-five or older. Many households had children, and the average family's income in 1972 fell between \$10,000 and \$25,000, with the majority making over \$15,000. Residents said they moved to North Palm Beach for various reasons, but most of them stated that it was a good place to raise kids and that the area's homes had plenty of space. They also said the appearance of the community, as well as their neighbors, made the village a pleasant place to live. Of all the residents in North Palm Beach, 44 percent had moved to the area from another state.

As of this book's publication date, North Palm Beach looks like this:

- In 2018, the estimated population of North Palm Beach was 13,129.
- About 92 percent of North Palm Beach's residents are white, and only about 3.9 percent are African American or Black. Hispanic or Latinos made up 10.4 percent of the population, and Asians made up 1.5 percent.
- A majority of the population is sixty-five years old or older.
- From 2013 to 2017, the median household income was \$59,905, and during that time, 7 percent of the village's population was living in poverty.

The history of the village is subtle but present. And while it may appear like any other town to outsiders, North Palm Beach has its own unique personality. To understand the history of the village, one must look farther back—to the beginnings of human settlement in an area that would one day become northern Palm Beach County.

Chapter 1

RICH ONLY BY THE SEA

The King of Ais and the King of Jeaga are poor Indians, as respects the land; for there are no mines of silver or of gold where they are; and, in short, they are rich only by the sea…

—Memoir of d'Escalante Fontaneda: Respecting Florida, *written in Spain, circa 1575*

First Glance at Florida

In 1575, the first memoir to describe early Florida was written by Hernando d'Escalante Fontaneda. At age thirteen—around 1549—Fontaneda was traveling to Spain to pursue his studies with his brother when their ship wrecked in the Florida Keys. The native Calusa tribe took them captive, and Fontaneda appears to have been the lone survivor. There is still some uncertainty about the specific date of the wreck, and no one is sure where in the Keys the wreck occurred.

Fontaneda wrote that he'd been captured as a boy by the Calusa, but he was rescued at age thirty by Pedro Menéndez de Avilés, who is mostly remembered for founding St. Augustine. He spent seventeen years in captivity and provided the first documentation of the Calusa villages, including Tampa on the west coast of Florida, in his memoir. He mentioned the Jeaga and Ais Florida tribes, who resided on the east coast, but he never actually interacted with them. Jonathan Dickinson and his party, however, met the Jeaga near Jupiter Inlet on the east coast of Florida more than one hundred years after Fontaneda's memoir was written.

Jonathan Dickinson and the Jeaga

On August 23, 1696, Jonathan Dickinson, a Quaker merchant, left Jamaica on a ship bound for Philadelphia. His wife and baby traveled with him, along with the ship's crew, a missionary, a relative of Dickinson's and eleven slaves. Though they'd been a part of a convoy, the ship became separated from the others. On September 22, a bad storm hit, and their ship, *Reformation*, was run aground. Everyone managed to get to shore about five miles north of Jupiter Inlet.

Dickinson wrote, "About the eighth or ninth hour came two Indian men (being naked except a small piece of platted work of straws which just hid their private parts, and fastened behind with a horsetail in likeness made of a sort of silk-grass) from the southward, running fiercely and foaming at the mouth having no weapons except their knives…" According to Dickinson's writings, the chief of the tribe stripped the prisoners, took everything they had and marched them to the south, where they were taken to the village at the inlet. Because the Jeaga had a better relationship with the Spanish than they did with the English, Dickinson and the others decided to pretend to be Spaniards. He wrote, "And one of us named Solomon Cresson, speaking the Spanish language well, it was hoped this might be a means for our delivery, to which most of the company assented." Though their fate always seemed uncertain, Dickinson wrote that when his wife had run out of breast milk, the Native women helped sustain the child by nursing it.

After holding them captive for several days, the tribe chose to free them. After leaving the tribe, Dickinson and his fellow travelers moved north, to Saint Augustine. They eventually reached their destination, Philadelphia, where Dickinson raised his family, became active in local politics, served twice as mayor of the city and lived out the rest of his years. He died in 1722.

In the days of these early Florida travelers, the Jeaga natives resided in and around the geographical location of present-day North Palm Beach. It is believed that the largest Jeaga village was located in the area that is now known as Riviera Beach, just south of present-day North Palm Beach and Lake Park.

The Riviera Beach Mound

In 1901, a scientist named Charles Newcomb purchased a hotel in Riviera Beach that had been built on a Native American shell mound or midden mound. The site is now known as the Riviera Beach Archaeological Complex, even though it has long since been demolished to make way for development. Previously, there was nothing to protect such historic locations, and it is easy to assume that most people who moved to Florida around the time of its demolition didn't recognize the historical and anthropological importance of these mounds.

Charles Newcomb, however, was intrigued by the mound. In 1914, when he lived in Florida, Newcomb drew a sketch of what was left of the narrow mound. It extended for five blocks, from West Park Drive to the shore of Lake Worth. Another Jeaga mound still exists beneath the DuBois Pioneer Home, a historic house less than ten miles north of North Palm Beach; it was built on top of the mound in 1898. The location of the DuBois Pioneer Home is probably where the Jeaga took Dickinson when they captured his party.

The area that is now known as North Palm Beach was a wilderness populated by natives, as evidenced by these mounds. Evidence of their presence has also been found in the vicinity of John D. MacArthur Beach State Park.

An Unknown People

Human history in Florida goes back for thousands of years. Historians have stated that ancient Europeans reached North America by walking across a narrow, frozen part of the Pacific Ocean called Beringia. They eventually traveled down to Florida, and DNA evidence that has been recovered from the state's burial ponds, such as the Windover site near Titusville, show that the natives who lived there were European in origin.

Very little is known about the Jeaga beyond the evidence that has been recovered from the mounds and European accounts such as Dickinson's journal. Archaeological findings have revealed that the natives ate a lot of shellfish. Certain items recovered from mounds—such as flint, which wasn't naturally found in South Florida—indicate that the Jeaga traded with northern tribes. Florida is home to many important archeological sites, and they each tell the stories of the Native American tribes that were wiped out after the arrival of the Spanish. Many of Florida's natives couldn't withstand the diseases the Spanish explorers brought with them, including smallpox.

While we know very little about the natives who lived in the area of North Palm Beach, we can imagine what their lives must have been like based on the food they ate and the items they traded with neighboring tribes. There is no visible evidence of their presence in North Palm Beach, Lake Park or Riviera Beach today, but they remain a part of northern Palm Beach County's hidden history.

Chapter 2

FROM WAR TO THE EXPLORATION OF PARADISE

Indeed, Florida was the Indian's paradise…of little value to us.
—Lieutenant William T. Sherman

Forty-Two Years of War in Florida

With a bit of imagination, we can visualize what the area of present-day northern Palm Beach County might have looked like in the late 1800s. People traveled by train and, later, by steamer to reach South Florida. Nearly every trace of the original Native American population was gone. The tribes had been effectively wiped out during Florida's two hundred years of Spanish rule, but they were replaced by newcomers who would eventually be known as the Seminoles.

While the Seminoles' early history is intertwined with that of the Creek tribes, whose members lived in what is now Georgia and Alabama, their story is complex and spans many years. It also connects them with the earlier Florida tribes, whose members they consider to be their ancestors. As the aboriginal tribes of Florida died out, Native Americans from Georgia and Alabama moved farther south and began cohabitating with the remaining members of the first Floridians. Over the years, these Native Americans built a cultural identity that was separate from the Creeks and became known as Seminoles. Many runaway slaves—called Maroons—joined and inter-married with the Seminoles. Some were held as slaves by Seminole leaders. However, black people and Seminoles had a common enemy that unified them—they were fighting for their freedom.

In 1817, the United States government sent General Andrew Jackson into Florida to respond to the cross-border violence between the Seminoles and Georgian settlers. Jackson's purpose was to punish the Native Americans and capture any runaway slaves. This action sparked the First Seminole War. Jackson also took the initiative to capture the Spanish capital of Pensacola. This eventually led to the Spanish cession of Florida to the United States in 1821. In 1830, Congress passed the Indian Removal Act, which prompted the government to forcibly move Native Americans to areas west of the Mississippi—mainly Oklahoma. When the Seminoles refused to leave Florida, the Second Seminole War began and lasted from 1835 to 1842. It was one of the most expensive and bloody wars that the United States waged against Native Americans. The Third Seminole War unfolded in the 1850s, when the United States attempted to remove the rest of the tribe. The Seminoles refused to give up and earned the right to call themselves "unconquered."

During these forty-two years of war, the soldiers who served in Florida built forts and created roads, including Military Trail, which was constructed by soldiers during the Third Seminole War. Cities were formed around these military installations, and the area's geographic features, including Lake Worth and Dade County, were named after officers in the army.

While the North Palm Beach area was never the site of any notable conflict between the Seminoles and the United States military during the Seminole Wars, it was continually patrolled from 1838 to 1842 and again during the Third Seminole War. Two major battles were fought in nearby Jupiter, where there were also several Native American villages. The battles took place in January 1838 at what is now Loxahatchee Battlefield Park and Riverbend Park, which are located west of Interstate 95 on State Road 706. The first battle was led by Lieutenant Levin Powell of the U.S. Navy and resulted in his defeat. The second battle was led by General Thomas Jesup and had no clear victor.

EARLY TRAVEL AND THE CELESTIAL RAILROAD

In 1866, what we now know as Palm Beach County was part of Dade County, which was very large and stretched south, past Miami and into the Florida Keys. The county seat was in Miami, and this caused a lot of difficulty for

Construction of the railroad at the Jupiter Inlet between 1890 and 1895. *State Library of Florida.*

the residents in the northern end of the county. If they wanted to conduct any official business or vote in any elections, they had to travel for quite a distance. The Celestial Railroad (the Jupiter and Lake Worth Railway) replaced a stagecoach that brought passengers from the Jupiter dock to Lake Worth. From 1889, when the Celestial Railroad first opened, to 1895, when the railway shut down, it conducted a thirty-minute run between Jupiter and Juno. When it was time to return to Jupiter, the train had to travel backward, as it couldn't turn around. Some evidence of the railway can still be found in the Twelve Oaks community of North Palm Beach, which is located near the intersection of PGA Boulevard and U.S. Highway 1.

In the nineteenth century, reaching the shores of Lake Worth from Jacksonville involved taking a steamer and a mule-drawn wagon to Titusville. From there, passengers would board a sailboat to Jupiter. This leg of the journey sometimes took weeks to complete. Once they reached Jupiter, passengers could either row through eight miles of sawgrass or travel ten miles by sea.

After much deliberation, the decision was made to move the county seat from Miami to Juno. The residents from the northern end of the county

The Jupiter and Lake Worth Railway (Celestial Railroad) steam engine. *State Library of Florida.*

outvoted those from the southern end. Dade County covered a lot of ground, and in 1890, its entire population was just 257 people. The one-acre lot that was reserved for the courthouse and county seat was donated by a man named Albert M. Field, and the construction of the new building was completed in 1889. It stood on the northeast corner of what is now U.S. Highway 1 and PGA Boulevard. The land was only occupied by trees, sand, wilderness and the two-story courthouse where the county judge and sheriff operated. This is what the northern end of the county looked like in the late 1800s—after the Seminole Wars ended in 1858.

In 1899, the county seat was moved back to Miami. Old Juno—the area surrounding PGA Boulevard, which takes up part of what is now North Palm Beach and Palm Beach Gardens—once again became a wilderness when a fire destroyed much of what had been built there. The railway stops between Jupiter and Juno were eventually forgotten, but people had already begun purchasing land in what would later become the Village of North Palm Beach.

At this time, the area that is now known as Palm Beach County was part of various other counties, beginning in 1821, when it was part of St. Johns County. Palm Beach County was founded in 1909. The Celestial Railroad shut down after Henry Flagler came through the area with a new railroad that connected more Floridian communities. After 1917, the Dixie Highway, which ran alongside Flagler's railroad, made it possible for farmers to transport their harvests to West Palm Beach, where they could then be sold. The county lines were officially set in 1925, when Martin County was formed to the north.

Why the Celestial Railroad?

To understand the origins of the Celestial Railroad's name, one should first understand Florida's early history. When Spain ceded Florida to the British, it became a British territory and remained that way from 1763 to 1784. The British saw Jobe (pronounced Ho-bay) on Spanish maps. Jobe was the name of a Jeaga village. The name reminded the British of "Jove"—the Roman name for Zeus—so they altered it to their version of the same name, which was Jupiter. The town of Juno was given its name later on. In Greek mythology, Juno is the queen of the gods. Mars and Venus were added as stops in keeping with this theme. Thus, the Celestial Railroad was born.

The First Land Owners in North Palm Beach

General land office records from the U.S. Department of Interior name the early land patents that were located in the vicinity of what is now North Palm Beach. In 1883, Dr. John Alexander Anders and Dr. Stephen Bennett Bell, who were both from Leon County, Florida, made several land purchases in the areas of North Palm Beach and Juno. An article published in the April 18, 1901 edition of the *Weekly Tallahasseean* stated that Dr. Anders owned a pineapple farm "on the east coast." The Juno area was the site of many pineapple farms in the late 1800s, so it is possible that he purchased land there to farm pineapples. Between the two men, they purchased four lots in the same section of land—where the North Palm Beach Country Club now stands—and three lots in Juno. In total, they purchased over 280 acres. The majority of this land was in modern-day North Palm Beach, and the document that lists the lots near the country club was issued on April 30, 1883.

Dr. Anders married Hester Newell Cromartie, and Dr. Bell married Hester's sister, Rebecca Carolyne Cromartie. Both men served as Confederate soldiers during the Civil War. After the war, Anders went on to practice dentistry. He also became a farmer and served Leon County, Florida, as a county commissioner. He was born on September 12, 1834, in North Carolina and died at age seventy-four on June 21, 1909, in Leon County, Florida. Dr. Anders and Hester had seven children.

A cousin of the Cromarties, Augustus Cromartie, moved to Juno in the late 1890s—perhaps after being inspired by Dr. Anders. Though the Anders family owned land in what is now northern Palm Beach County, they lived in Iamonia in Leon County. In 1959, *Fort Lauderdale News* printed a story that said:

> *Augustus Cromartie loaded his family into a covered wagon at Auburndale, near Lakeland, in 1896 and went in search of a tomato country below the frostline. They emerged from the pathless woods at Jupiter, where there was no bridge. Taking the wagon apart, they ferried it across by rowboat, towing the horse behind. The Celestial Railroad had been abandoned after the FEC built through, but its wooden rails still were in place. The Cromarties' effects were loaded on a tram car, and their horse pulled it to Juno.*

Stephen Bell served the Confederacy as a corporal and was later promoted to sergeant. He was described as being five foot six inches tall, with a sallow complexion, grey eyes and dark hair. Bell was also listed as a physician in the 1870 U.S. Census. He was born on September 11, 1844, and died on August 4, 1896. Though neither Bell nor Anders ever resided in what was then Dade County, they are both given the distinction of likely being the first private landowners in North Palm Beach.

In 1892, when both Anders and Bell were nearing the ends of their lives, the area that encompasses Lake Park and North Palm Beach—excluding the Anders-Bell properties—was given to Albert Sawyer in the form of a trust from the State of Florida. The trust stipulated that he had to "improve, cultivate or sell the land before 1907." When he died in 1903, the land was given to his son, Albert Sawyer Jr., who sold the land to Barton Peck in 1915 for a total of $1,140. It was then sold to Harry Kelsey for $100,000 in 1919.

Prairie Siding and Prosperity Farming Settlements

Besides old Juno, the first pioneer settlements near North Palm Beach were located in what is now Palm Beach Gardens. They were all near the intersection of Alternate A1A and PGA Boulevard. Prosperity Farms Road, which runs through North Palm Beach, and Monet Road, are the only existing nods to these settlements.

Prairie, or Prairie Siding, was located near a railway stop. The minutes from the directors meeting of the West Palm Beach Library, which were published on August 8, 1919, show the existence of a library built specifically

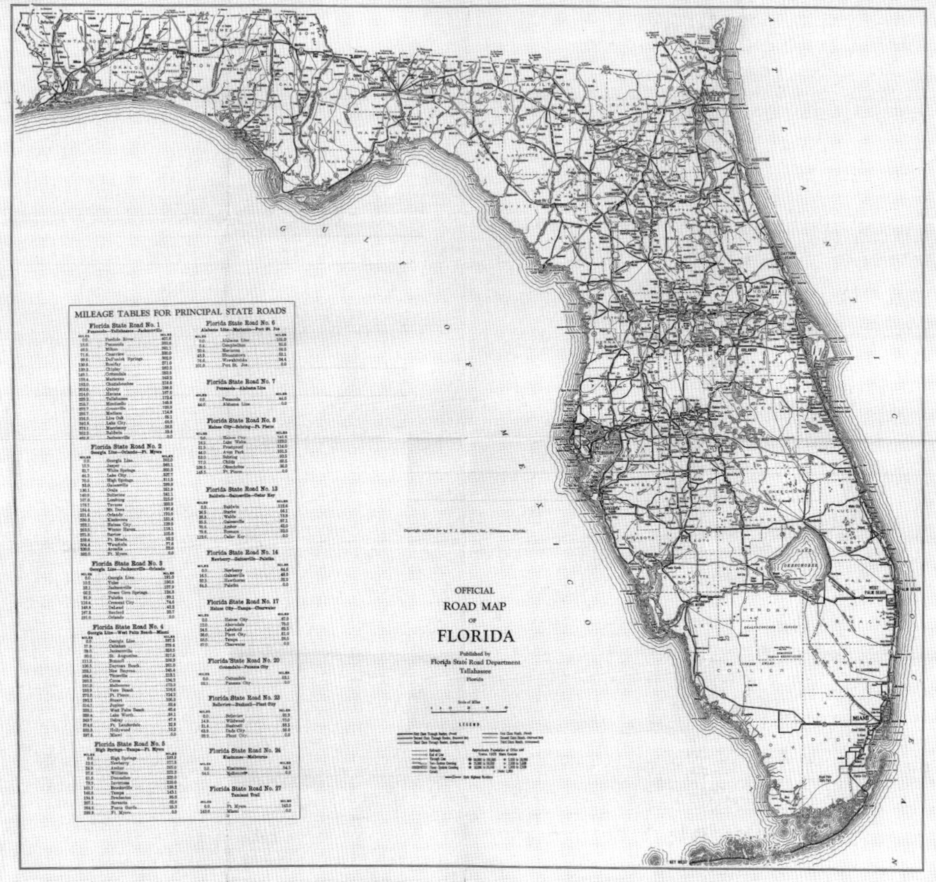

This 1930 road map shows Kelsey City and Prairie. The farming settlements of Prairie and Prosperity, later Monet, were once located in the area of present-day Palm Beach Gardens. *State Library of Florida.*

for the community in Prairie: "[The librarian] reported the donation of some books to the Prairie Siding library, the books donated being duplicates of those already on hand." There was also a small schoolhouse in the area. In 1920, the county superintendent reported that the Prairie Siding school at District No. 1 had ten pupils and one teacher, who was being paid a salary of $480.00 per year. The same county's superintendent's report shows that a second school in the same district was serving Prosperity Farms. This school had twenty students and one teacher, who was being paid a salary of $600.00 per year. The Prosperity Farms school was built "during the school year, closing June 30, 1920," according to a report published that year in the *Palm Beach Post*.

Children from Prairie Siding started attending the Prosperity School in the early 1920s, and news reports from the time seem to hint that the Prairie Siding school probably closed soon after. When Kelsey City Elementary was built in 1923, Prairie Siding's children were bused there instead. Prosperity was renamed Monet around 1924. The area's first wave of pioneers had succeeded in shaping this part of South Florida. The farming communities of Prairie Siding, Monet and Prosperity were absorbed into the surrounding towns as the development of the area progressed over the years.

Chapter 3

PIONEERS IN THE LAND OF ENCHANTMENT

Florida has ever been a land of romance....There is frequently a fringe of forest surrounding the shores. The blue of the sky is reflected in the water, until its depths seem of azure.
—Florida, the Land of Enchantment, *Nevin O. Winter, 1918*

The Wilson Family

Frank Wilson and his family had a farm in Prosperity. Frank, along with his wife and their eight children, moved to the area in 1923 from Tennessee, where he had managed a mercantile store in a mining town called Wilder. The business began losing money when the town's miners went on strike, so Frank had to find another way to support his large family. He eventually found his answer in South Florida.

Frank's brother was already living in West Palm Beach, and he talked him into moving there. When he arrived, Frank ran into an old friend, who sold him ten acres of land. When a hurricane hit the coast in 1928, it devastated much of south and central Florida. The Wilson family home was one casualty of the storm, and they had to rebuild. They chose a spot at the top of a hill, where today's Ellison Wilson Road is located. After Frank's son Ellison was killed in World War II, the road was named in his honor. Frank Wilson remained on the farm and lived well into his nineties.

The McLaren Family

McLaren Road is located on unincorporated land near the border of North Palm Beach. The family that the road is named after came to the area in 1915. Robert Edgar McLaren, a factory owner from up north, came to Florida on a short-term basis—at first. Like many travelers who were drawn to Florida's warmth, Robert's first goal was to recover from an illness. Once his health improved, he realized he liked Florida so much that he wanted to stay, so he sold all of his property and relocated. He built a house near the Intracoastal Waterway, and the rest of his family soon followed him.

By the time Robert and his wife had settled in Florida, they had ten children. They attempted to run a farm before he entered the construction business. Since the area they lived in was so remote, the McLarens had to take a boat to West Palm Beach in order to get supplies and pick up their mail (there was no mail delivery service at the time). In 1918, Robert built a little schoolhouse across the water from his family's home. The Monet drawbridge, which was built just south of the McLaren home by Palm Beach County, gave people a way to cross the waterway without boarding a boat.

Around 2005, North Palm Beach resident Charlotte Chickering, author of *The 50th Anniversary of the Village of North Palm Beach: An Official History*, interviewed Lulu McLaren-Nelson, who stated that one of her sisters worked as a toll collector for Harry Kelsey, the founder of Kelsey City. It was her job to unlatch the chain for any passing boats at the Monet bridge. During a hurricane, the bridge washed away, and it has never been rebuilt.

Harry Kelsey Dreams of Paradise

When Harry Kelsey arrived in Florida in 1919 to recover from pneumonia, he loved it so much that he decided to stay—much like Robert McLaren before him. He felt inspired by everything he saw and viewed the land as a great opportunity, so he purchased a large tract that now encompasses Lake Park, North Palm Beach and Palm Beach Gardens.

Kelsey started his career in Massachusetts, opening the first location of what became the Waldorf chain of restaurants. After discovering all of the possibilities available in Florida, Kelsey resigned from his business,

Harry Kelsey envisioned an idyllic community, where all the necessities of life would be within reach. He founded Kelsey City, which later became Lake Park, in 1919. *Lake Park Historical Society*.

opened East Coast Finance Corporation (so he could work in real estate) and began planning a city that he hoped would attract thousands and offer everything necessary to build a happy life. Kelsey's ideas for the city were filled with optimism. He envisioned an idyllic and prosperous community, and he had the tenacity and perseverance to see it come to fruition. Kelsey is remembered as an honest person who might have trusted people too easily.

Sixty thousand acres of land around what Kelsey dubbed Kelsey City were set aside for agriculture. In 1925, he bought out some of the farmers in the surrounding area and established a dairy. The dairy was located between present-day Prosperity Farms Road and Alternate A1A. It was one of the first in the area to offer local deliveries.

Kelsey built an observation tower so that prospective landowners could get a good view of what they would be purchasing. Lots in Kelsey City were sold by auction under an open-air tent. The Olmsted brothers, whose father successfully designed New York City's Central Park, were hired, along with Dr. John Nolan from Boston, to help set the stage for Florida's very first zoned municipality.

Kelsey City Golf Course

Kelsey also started building a golf course that was never fully completed. It was originally intended to be a standard eighteen-hole course, but only nine were ever finished. He first referred to this golf club as the Palm Beach Winter Club, but he later transferred this name to the mansion he and Paris Singer—one of the twenty-four children of Singer sewing machine magnate, Isaac Singer—constructed farther north. This first nine-hole course no longer exists.

On August 7, 1920, Kelsey met with golfer and course architect Donald Ross and the Olmsted brothers to discuss plans for the golf club in Kelsey City and the Kelsey City Golf Course. The course they built extended across the present-day intersection of Northlake Boulevard and U.S. Highway 1. According to the Lake Park Historical Society, part of the course was located a bit west of the present-day North Palm Beach Public Library. A wooden clubhouse stood in this location as well, according to an article published in the *Palm Beach Post*.

It is important to note that golfer Donald Ross is not the same person as Donald Alexander Ross, for whom Donald Ross Road was later named. Donald Alexander Ross was the first Lake Park resident to lose his life during World War II. He died in 1944 during the Battle of the Bulge.

STYMIE GAUGE—SIX INCHES

Do not Climb Bunker Faces. No Stroke but Putt allowed on Putting Green — Match Play Handicap is ¾ of Medal Play Handicap — Matches Playing More than 4 Balls Not Permitted — Any Match failing to hold its place MUST let following Match play through

Hole	Yds.	Check	Check	Hdc. Str.	Foursome Check Col.	Par	Check	Check	Ladies Par	Hole	Yds.	Check	Check	Hdc. Str.	Foursome Check Col.	Par	Check	Check	Ladies
1	440			5		4			5	1	440			5		4			
2	380			9		4			5	2	380			9		4			
3	170			1		3			3	3	170			1		3			
4	350			7		4			4	4	350			7		4			
5	530			2		5			6	5	530			2		5			
6	120			4		3			3	6	120			4		3			
7	415			8		4			5	7	415			8		4			
8	260			3		4			4	8	260			3		4			
9	470			6		5			5	9	470			6		5			
Gross	3135					36			40	In	3135					[illegible]			4
Hdc.										Out	3135					36			4
Net										Total	6270					72			8
Scorer Signature										Hdc.									
Attest					Date					Net									

Be a Sportsman. Observe the U. S. G. A. Rules and Etiquette of Golf. PLEASE REPLACE TURF. High-heeled shoes must not be worn on the course.

Top: The Kelsey City Golf Course was dubbed the Palm Beach Winter Club several years before the second Winter Club was built next to the present-day North Palm Beach Country Club. This nine-hole course, shown on the back of a score card, was located near the intersection of U.S. Highway 1 and Northlake Boulevard, and it extended just west of the North Palm Beach Public Library. *Lake Park Historical Society*.

Bottom: The score card from the Kelsey City Golf Course shows the course's nine holes. *Lake Park Historical Society*.

The Everglades Club and Paris Singer

Paris Eugene Singer, born on February 20, 1867, was the son of Isaac Singer, an inventor and the founder of the Singer Sewing Machine Company. Before coming to Florida, Paris was educated at Cambridge University. He first visited Florida in 1917 and later decided to purchase land there. He built the Touchstone Convalescents' Home as a hospital for soldiers wounded in World War I. The building was designed by noted architect Addison Mizner, who arrived in Florida in 1918 when Singer hired him. The war ended before the home could be utilized, and Singer opened the building in 1919 as the private, exclusive Everglades Club.

Paris Singer was connected to another notable individual: He had a long-term love affair with the beautiful dancer Isadora Duncan, who was born around 1877 in California. She met Paris after one of her shows

Paris Eugene Singer. *State Library of Florida.*

in France. They had a child together but were never married. In 1927, when Isadora died after an automobile accident in France—one of her famous scarves got caught in the axle of her car—it was Paris who made the arrangements for her funeral.

In the early 1920s, Paris teamed up with Harry Kelsey to build the Winter Club, which was located next to the site of today's North Palm Beach Country Club. They anticipated the Winter Club would be just as successful as the Everglades Club in Palm Beach.

Seth Raynor Designs the Golf Course at the Winter Club

Harry Kelsey and Paris Singer spent $500,000 building the club and golf course, which they completed in 1926. Singer hosted the opening of the brand-new eighteen-hole course in what is now North Palm Beach. The course, which was designed by Seth Raynor, seemed like a natural addition to the area due to the success of the course at the Everglades Club. The December 31, 1925 edition of the *Palm Beach Post* stated, "Mr. Seth J. Raynor, the well-known golf architect of Southampton, has laid out the course in the same subtle and masterly way he laid out our present nine-hole course eight years ago, and I feel sure it will be up to his usual high standards." The nine-hole course mentioned in the article was likely the course at the Everglades Club, one of Raynor's most well-known local golf courses.

Raynor had been taught by Charles Blair Macdonald, who is considered the father of golf course design and architecture. Macdonald, Raynor and another designer named Charles Banks are credited with creating the design template that has been followed by other golf course designers. Ironically, Raynor was a surveyor and civil engineer who had no interest in golfing himself, but he was responsible for designing many well-known courses.

The course at the Winter Club was located six miles north of Palm Beach. Locals could easily access the course by water or by traveling down the Dixie Highway through what was then called Kelsey City. The course could also be reached by traveling down "the new Ocean boulevard running through Palm Beach and up to Jupiter," or the state road that was being built at the time to connect Jacksonville to Miami.

The Winter Club was dedicated as a clubhouse on March 26, 1927, but Seth Raynor had already passed away from pneumonia in West Palm Beach on January 22, 1926. He did not get to see the success of his golf course. The first owners who paid their dues at the North Palm Beach Winter Club were B.D. Cole of B.D. Cole Insurance Company and Robert C. Baker.

Mules housed in Kelsey City helped plow and prepare the land for the golf course at the second Winter Club around 1926. This building once stood next to the present-day North Palm Beach Country Club. *Lake Park Historical Society.*

LOUIS DE PUYSEGER, DESIGNER OF THE WINTER CLUB BUILDING

At one time, the Palm Beach Winter Club was going to be called "the new Everglades Club," but the name was changed to avoid confusion with Singer's club on Palm Beach. The success of the Everglades Club was certainly one of the inspirations behind the construction of the Winter Club, and a number of wealthy visitors attended its grand opening.

Louis De Puyseger, a friend of Paris Singer, was hired to design the building in the Mediterranean Revival style of architecture. According to a 1928 advertisement in the *Palm Beach Post*, "George A. Hoffman, professional, will be in charge of golf activities. The dining room service will be in charge of Miss M.I. Falconer. Bridge entertainments, afternoon teas as well as evening dinner parties, will be accommodated. By reservation."

Above: The Winter Club, which was built by Harry Kelsey and Paris Singer in 1926, once stood beside the present-day North Palm Beach Country Club. This photograph was taken between 1935 and 1939. It shows the 1935 addition, built by Harry Oakes, which is visible on the left side of the photo at the back of the building. *Village of North Palm Beach.*

Opposite: Visiting tourists could arrange to take a bus from Palm Beach to the Winter Club. This photograph was taken between the late 1940s and early 1950s. *Village of North Palm Beach.*

Down Where the Paw-Paw Grows

At one time, one of Harry Kelsey's plans for Kelsey City involved a golf course and a resort on Munyon Island, which would have connected the two locations, but this plan never came to fruition. The island was once home to a large number of pelicans, and in the 1880s, a man named Rogers also lived there, subsisting on fruit from the island's trees. He also sold green turtles to passersby.

Before it was known as Munyon's Island, the land was owned by Nathan W. Pitts and was referred to as Pitts Island. Nathan built a house there, and since he and his wife enjoyed horticulture, they turned the island into a paradise of flora, for which it became quite well known.

Later, Munyon Island was named after Dr. James Munyon, who bought the island and opened a health resort there. He was also the owner of a company called Munyon's Proprietary Medicines in Philadelphia, Pennsylvania. While Munyon did not actually hold a doctoral degree, his "medicine"—Dr. Munyon's Paw-Paw tonic—was promoted as a rejuvenating tonic that could be used for just about anything. The main ingredient of the elixir was actually fermented papaya juice. "With this medicine, there is hope," Munyon claimed. To help market his elixir, he wrote a catchy tune called "Down Where the Paw-Paw Grows."

Munyon's Isle all hearts beguile
Down where the paw-paw grows
There's joy for each at gay Palm Beach
Down where the paw-paw grows.

He also claimed that one of his island's attractions was a "fountain of youth," but the fountain only turned out regular water piped from the mainland.

In the early 1900s, Dr. Munyon already had a popular hotel on his island—the Hygeia. In 1917, the hotel burned down, and Munyon sold the land to Kelsey for $65,000. Dr. Munyon died the following year. Although Kelsey had a lot of ideas for the island, they all disintegrated. In 1926, the estate sued Kelsey for his failure to pay for the island, and they took it back. Kelsey refocused his attentions elsewhere, namely on the Winter Club and golf course north of Kelsey City.

A MANMADE PARADISE

Peanut Island, formally known as Inlet Island, was the direct result of dredging and development. In 1918, Lake Worth Inlet was deepened, and the leftovers were dumped into Lake Worth, which made for an unintentional piece of manmade land. The Port of Palm Beach continued to use the island to maintain the inlet, and the name was changed to Peanut Island when the State of Florida allowed it to be used as a terminal for peanut oil shipments. The name stuck, but the plan didn't. Peanut oil shipping was eventually abandoned.

In 1936, a coast guard station was built on the island, and in 1961, during the Cuban Missile Crisis, a secret bunker was constructed there to protect President Kennedy and his family in the event of an emergency. Thankfully, it was never needed for this purpose. Both Munyon Island and Peanut Island grew in size during the 1990s, when the Intracoastal Waterway was dredged. The piling up of sand and detritus doubled the size of Munyon Island from its original fifteen acres.

LOCAL TRAVEL AND THE PARKER BRIDGE

A few things changed in the mid-1920s that altered the way people traveled locally; it also changed the areas in which travelers stopped and visited. Once

U.S. Highway 1 was constructed between 1926 and 1927, tourists were able to take a shuttle from Palm Beach to play golf at the Winter Club in what would later become North Palm Beach.

The Parker Bridge was also built in 1926 on U.S. Highway 1, north of the present-day country club. Earnest Parker, who was born on August 20, 1867, had been working for the Florida state road department when he took a job as a bridge tender. Parker and his wife, Mary Jane, lived in a little house near the bridge. The bridge itself had to be operated manually, so Parker was on the clock at all hours of the day. One of his sixteen grandchildren, Francis Parker Rines, recalled spending winters with her grandparents as a child, playing by the water where her grandfather loyally maintained his post.

The Florida Land Bust

Despite Harry Kelsey's initial success, Florida's economy began to crumble in 1925. The Florida land boom of the 1920s had passed, and the bust was underway. Kelsey went bankrupt while trying to rebuild the town after the hurricane in 1928, which devastated the area. He sold the Winter Club and surrounding lands to Sir Harry Oakes before returning to the North in 1929. The stock market crash that year, and the onset of the Great Depression, meant there was no recovery from the land bust. In 1932, Paris Singer died in England from heart attack, having permanently made his mark in Florida.

The Village Legend of Harry Oakes

Sir Harry Oakes was born on December 23, 1874, and grew up in Sangerville, Maine. He attended two years of medical school after graduating from Bowdoin College in New England, but he eventually abandoned his education in order to pursue wealth. In his early twenties, Oakes went searching for gold. In 1911, he prospected for over a year in Canada and opened a mine. He became a multi-millionaire in 1921. In the 1930s, when Canadian taxes became too much for him, he left and headed to the Bahamas, but he retained the property he had purchased from Harry Kelsey in northern Palm Beach County. The land encompassed what is now Lake

Park, Palm Beach Shores, Palm Beach Gardens and North Palm Beach, and it included the Winter Club on U.S. Highway 1. Oakes had constructed horse stables on the property for his eldest daughter, Nancy, and he built an addition to the Winter Club in 1935. Though the family owned the Winter Club and the surrounding land, they didn't reside in the area full-time.

When Alfred "Freddie" de Marigny of Nassau became involved with Nancy, Oakes didn't approve of the relationship. Freddie was in his late thirties and Nancy had just turned eighteen when they eloped. In 1943, Harry Oakes was murdered in the Bahamas. His body was found in his bed, burned beyond recognition, and the murder was never solved. Despite the fact that Oakes's murder had occurred far from the Winter Club, the local children of North Palm Beach were enthralled by the story and imagined Oakes's ghost roaming around the old building. Christine Schwencke, daughter of developer Jack Schwencke, grew up in North Palm Beach and recalled how local children would tell ghost stories about Harry Oakes. "His widow was left with all this property…so, supposedly, his ghost still went around the Winter Club."

Though Freddie de Marigny was arrested and charged with Sir Harry Oakes's murder, Nancy supported her husband's claims that he had nothing to do with it. He was acquitted in November 1943. Photos of the old Winter Club add to the mystique of the area's history and its memorable characters of the early twentieth century. Harry Kelsey, Paris Singer and Harry Oakes continue to capture the imaginations of North Palm Beach's residents.

Chapter 4

MILLIONAIRES AND DEVELOPERS STEP INTO THE WILDERNESS

MacArthur was [very] *eccentric. He put in PGA Boulevard, and he enticed the Professional Golfers Association to come here.*
—Christine Schwencke, daughter of North Palm Beach developer Jack Schwencke

JOHN D. MACARTHUR GOES TO FLORIDA

John D. MacArthur was born on March 6, 1897, the oldest child of seven. MacArthur's parents, William and Georgiana, started their life together as farmers, but William's true passion was ministry. The family didn't have much money, and William was often away from home, traveling as a minister. Growing up with so little probably sparked John MacArthur's desire for affluence in adulthood. He earned his fortune in the insurance industry of Chicago. He entered the business in 1935, when he purchased a company that was in financial trouble—Bankers Life and Casualty—for $2,500. After attaining success, he went on to purchase other small businesses and brought them up from near financial ruin. Known for his eccentricities and remembered as a person who was both persuasive and persistent, MacArthur often got what he wanted.

When MacArthur saw the same opportunities for development and expansion in Florida, he acquired 2,600 acres of land in Palm Beach County in 1954. According to an article in the *Palm Beach Post* from 1964, "In 1954, the Tesdem properties were sold to a group headed by Ralph Stolkin of

Chicago. Later, John D. MacArthur took control of the property and launched his North Palm Beach and Palm Beach Gardens developments." Apparently, Ralph Stolkin owed MacArthur money, but rather than make a payment, he chose to simply give up the land.

In May 1955, MacArthur went public with his plans to develop land in Palm Beach County. He intended to erect hotels, a golf and yacht club and thousands of homes. At that time, the land just north of Lake Park was mostly empty, with the exception of the old Winter Club, which once stood next to the present-day North Palm Beach Country Club. MacArthur's vision was to create a community that offered waterfront-centered living, and he wanted to plan it in a way that would attract higher-income families. To carry out his plan, he needed the local utilities to fit the community. Lake Park had cesspools, and according to MacArthur, it needed an updated utility system.

When he ran into opposition in 1955, he made official moves to dissolve the town of Lake Park. He claimed that he'd received no city services, despite owning about 85 percent of the land in Lake Park and paying $35,000 in taxes to the town. He also said Lake Park's water system was leaky and needed to be repaired or replaced. Without proper utilities, he couldn't continue on with his plans to develop. MacArthur negotiated to purchase Lake Park's system, redo the water mains and install a new sewer system.

His representative in these dealings was Charles Cunningham, president of the Palm Beach County Utilities Company. Cunningham represented MacArthur's interests in Chicago and spent over twenty-five years as a realtor in Chicago before moving to Palm Beach County in 1953. The legal battle between MacArthur and Lake Park went on for some time before they finally announced, in 1955, that they were close to reaching a compromise. Work began on Lake Park's new sewage and water systems in 1956—the same year the village was incorporated—and Cunningham became the first mayor of North Palm Beach. When North Palm Beach was incorporated in 1956, the land was technically still a part of Lake Park, and it remained that way until 1961.

At the groundbreaking of the new Lake Park water and sewer system, Charles Cunningham addressed attendees and stated that any past differences between MacArthur and the town of Lake Park had been resolved. Several town commissioners attended the ceremonial groundbreaking, along with a representative of the engineering firm, the secretary of the Palm Beach County Utilities Company and one man who was deeply involved in the planning and development of the Village of North Palm Beach—Richard "Dick" Ross.

THE ROSS BROTHERS AND JAY H. WHITE

By the time the Ross brothers, known to most as Dick and Bob Ross, began planning and constructing homes in what is now North Palm Beach, they had already built a solid reputation as home builders in West Palm Beach. Benefits from the GI Bill allowed veterans who were returning from World War II and the Korean War to readjust to civilian life and provide for their families. The Ross Construction Company built low-cost homes to serve the veteran population. These homes were popular and solid, and veterans were able to use the GI Bill to purchase them.

Margaret and Norman Robson were close friends of the Ross brothers. The couple was married in 1953 in West Palm Beach and moved to North Palm Beach in 1962. Margaret recalled that the Rosses were selling modest, well-built houses to veterans. Before she and her husband met the Rosses, they coincidentally purchased one of the brothers' homes in West Palm Beach. It was their first house as a married couple.

> *The government had given those vets of World War II* [help to buy a house]....*The Rosses were building houses with a down payment from the GI Bill. My husband was a veteran of World War II, and shortly after we were married, we plunked down Norm's* [money] *and bought one of their three-bedroom houses in West Palm Beach and thought it was the most wonderful thing in the world.*

Margaret recalled:

> [The Rosses] *had been builders in the south end of West Palm Beach.... Then they bought this large tract of land from John D. MacArthur* [which would later become North Palm Beach]. *They developed it, put in all these canals so there would be a lot of waterfront property for sale, which made it a very lucrative place to live.*

Margaret remembered the Ross brothers as people who were fun to be around. She also recalled her well-known Palm Beach friends, Anita and Bill Blakeslee, who were, according to the *Palm Beach Post*, "believed to be the first married couple to pass the Florida bar exam together."

Herbert "Bob" Ross was born on April 4, 1918. His brother, Richard "Dick" Ross, studied architecture at Pratt Institute, while Bob served as a lieutenant commander in the navy during World War II. Additionally, Bob had the distinction of being a civil rights activist. Together, they opened Ross Construction Company in 1946 and began their careers in construction in Dade and Broward Counties before turning their attention to West Palm Beach four years later.

In 1951, the Ross brothers and their brother-in-law, Jay H. White, registered the business name "Ross & White" with the clerk of the circuit court of Palm Beach County. Jay H. White, who was born in 1915, was a wealthy man who invested thousands of dollars in the development of the North Palm Beach area as a co-founder of the town.

JACK SCHWENCKE AND NORTH PALM BEACH PROPERTIES INC.

North Palm Beach Properties Inc. first filed as a for-profit corporation on June 23, 1955; its president and director was John A. Schwencke, who was also known as Jack Schwencke. John "Jack" Schwencke was born in 1917 in New York to John William and Margaret Theresa Schwencke. He attended Brooklyn Prep School, New York University and began a career in banking before he went into the United States Army. After serving in Europe during World War II, Schwencke moved to Florida and started a new career in real estate.

Schwencke was well-known and loved for his friendly demeanor, and he is remembered for his ability to make deals on a handshake alone. During his career, Schwencke also worked with Mr. William Blakeslee, and they, along with seven others, opened an investment company to help small businesses in 1959. This new business was referred to as "Greater SBIC of Florida." When Schwencke first opened his business in Hollywood, Florida, he met Dick and Bob Ross. He later joined them in West Palm Beach to work on what would become a very successful collaboration. From 1950 to 1956, the trio worked together to build thousands of homes in the West Palm Beach area.

Schwencke then founded North Palm Beach with the Ross brothers and Jay H. White; this was just the beginning of the group's collaboration. They purchased about 970 acres of land from John D. MacArthur, who, at one point, owned most of Lake Park. The transfer of the land—which was still a part of Lake Park—from MacArthur to Ross Construction Co. was announced in July 1955, and the group started laying the groundwork for the village in 1956. The town was incorporated in August 1956.

North Palm Beach Utilities Company

With the development of North Palm Beach on the horizon, MacArthur also signed a contract with the Rosses to build a water system and sewage plant. The Ross brothers built the North Palm Beach Sewage Plant and the water treatment plant; both facilities were designed by Brockway, Weber & Brockway Inc., and they both used features that were ordinarily found in much larger plants. The Ross brothers' plan was to look far enough into the future that any potential pitfalls could be avoided.

When the Ross brothers and their partners bought the land, MacArthur took out an option on the utility company that was owned by North Palm Beach Properties. North Palm Beach Utilities Company filed to become a corporation in July 1955. Jack Schwencke was its president and director, and Fred Trapnell served as its vice president. MacArthur eventually purchased North Palm Beach Utilities Company when the owners were unable to pay the bills, and he renamed it Seacoast Utilities. Schwencke remained on the staff of Seacoast, with MacArthur as a consultant, until he and John disagreed about the painting of a water tower on A1A. "It needed painting, so my dad had it painted for $300," Christine Schwencke recalled. "John D. called him into his office and said, 'Did I authorize the water tower being painted?' And he said, 'No, but it really needed it.'" MacArthur felt that $300 was too much to spend, so he fired Schwencke.

At one point, MacArthur entertained the idea of developing Munyon Island, but the Village of North Palm Beach objected. He fought them in court but failed, and now, Munyon Island is owned by the State of Florida—an undeveloped, yet popular, tourist attraction for boaters. The first village council in North Palm Beach consisted of Charles Cunningham, Dick Ross, Jay White, Jack Schwencke and Mr. MacArthur himself.

The Parade of Homes

Once model homes were constructed in North Palm Beach and all of the other essentials were in place, the "Parade of Homes" took place in 1956 and included seventeen houses. The event was sponsored by the Home Builders Association of Palm Beach County and was held in North Palm Beach, as the town was well-planned enough to avoid the usual issues new towns suffered as a result of unreliable utilities and unfinished business.

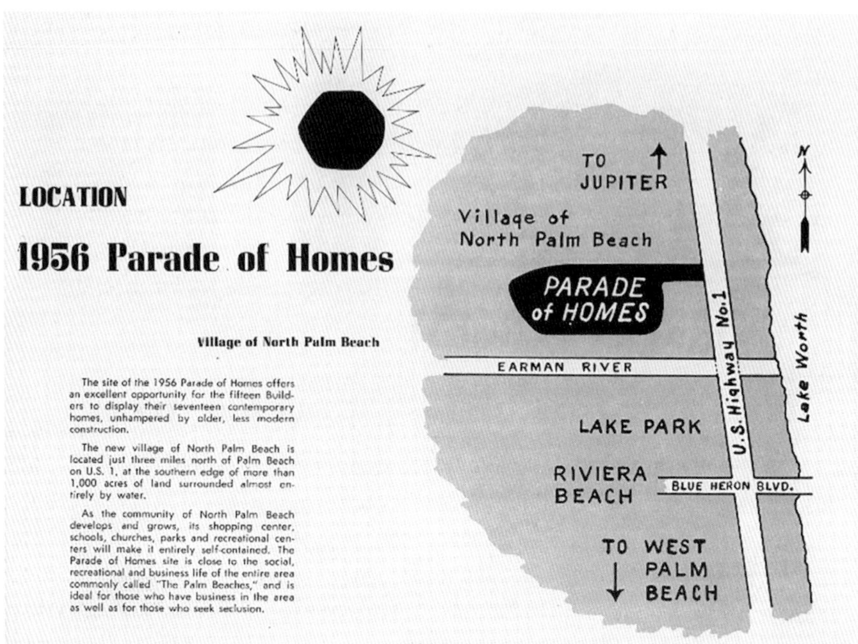

LOCATION

1956 Parade of Homes

Village of North Palm Beach

The site of the 1956 Parade of Homes offers an excellent opportunity for the fifteen Builders to display their seventeen contemporary homes, unhampered by older, less modern construction.

The new village of North Palm Beach is located just three miles north of Palm Beach on U.S. 1, at the southern edge of more than 1,000 acres of land surrounded almost entirely by water.

As the community of North Palm Beach develops and grows, its shopping center, schools, churches, parks and recreational centers will make it entirely self-contained. The Parade of Homes site is close to the social, recreational and business life of the entire area commonly called "The Palm Beaches," and is ideal for those who have business in the area as well as for those who seek seclusion.

This map shows the location of the 1956 Parade of Homes. *Village of North Palm Beach.*

North Palm Beach was carefully planned, and services were put in place before the first families moved in. This aerial photograph shows the construction of new homes in the late 1950s, when the village was expanding. *Village of North Palm Beach.*

Christine Schwencke remembered attending the Parade of Homes as a child.

> *It was just a small semicircle on South Anchorage Drive, and each builder had built different homes.... They had the fire engine out and the police cars out, and they gave away a lot of prizes, and they had games and things going on. It made people feel good when they moved here that everything was already in place. The streets were in place, streetlights, village hall, country club—there was a lot to move into. The place was already planned and mapped out, and the residents felt secure.*

A brochure for North Palm Beach contained a drawing that depicted a happy couple. The young woman is shown waving to passersby from a charming front yard. Early marketing and advertising materials about the village and its new homes spoke to families that may have been looking for a fresh, unspoiled paradise—a secure place to raise their children and put down roots. At the Parade of Homes, visitors could enter to win prizes, including a fifteen-foot-long Chris-Craft inboard runabout. Adults paid twenty-five cents to attend, and children under twelve years old were admitted for free.

Newly built homes in North Palm Beach, 1956. *Village of North Palm Beach.*

New homes in North Palm Beach, 1956. *Village of North Palm Beach.*

Other home builders were involved as well. Steve Higgins, who was born in September 1948 and who grew up in North Palm Beach, noted that his father, Norman Higgins—owner of Higgins Plastering Company—did a lot of work locally. On February 22, 1959, the North Palm Beach Chamber of Commerce hosted a "circus day" and published a brochure with a schedule of events, along with local builders' listings. Among them was Norman Higgins, who built his family's home on Harbour Road in 1958.

Chapter 5

BIRTH OF THE VILLAGE

From the very beginning, it was clear that North Palm Beach was to become a unique residential community. Superior planning almost guaranteed it, even before the village was launched.
—The 25th Anniversary of the Village of North Palm Beach: An Official History, *William Young, village historian*

A Town of Professional People

Much of the land between Lake Park and Jupiter had remained undeveloped and mostly untouched prior to MacArthur's arrival. The land that would become North Palm Beach reached north toward the Intracoastal Waterway and bordered the Earman Canal—later called the Earman River—to the south. There were a number of things that made this a prime area for development; chief among them was the fact that North Palm Beach had a ready-made country club in the form of the old Winter Club, also known as the Oakes Mansion. The Winter Club was a well-known local landmark.

In 1958, when Pratt & Whitney built a plant west of town, it was "a stroke of luck," according to Margaret Robson. Pratt & Whitney's arrival in South Florida attracted many new residents. Margaret said that when she and her husband first moved to North Palm Beach, most of their neighbors worked for Pratt & Whitney in some capacity. North Palm Beach was built for professional people. The town drew in doctors, engineers and teachers, and it became known as a good place for young couples to raise their children. The village was planned with careful consideration, and canals were dug to give residents easy access to the water. Before anyone moved in, the Rosses and their business partners thought of everything: public safety, a fire department, the town hall and public works. From 1964 to 1989, Herb Gildan served as the village attorney. He and his wife were also very involved in the community outside of his work.

PREPARED FOR FUTURE GROWTH

To offer waterfront properties in North Palm Beach, the canals had to be dredged. Captain Samuel T. Milling, a dredging contractor and the owner of Palm Beach Dredging Company, made this possible. Eleven wells were also dug around the village, and a water treatment plant was built west of town. The sewage treatment facility was constructed off Anchorage Drive. All of this work was done with future expansion in mind and accounted for the many families that they hoped would move into the village. The *Palm Beach Post* stated, "Instead of following the conventional pattern of erecting homes, the Ross brothers are first starting on $2,000,000 water and sewage disposal plants. This has been designed to service a population of 11,000, which is expected in that area within the next five years." Even the town's flood insurance plan covered the next forty years, ensuring the village would be well-equipped to handle future storms. The foundation of the village was set before the first family moved in. Just off U.S. Highway 1, to the west, there was a mucky area that developers chose to excavate. They used the fill to raise surrounding land, and this process created North and South Lake, which are both connected by the Earman River.

When Margaret Robson and her husband decided to move to North Palm Beach—after their friendship with the Ross brothers had blossomed—they purchased a waterfront lot from Dick and Bob, who gave them a special deal on the land. The couple paid the discounted cost offered to builders at the time. "We built this house, and my husband designed it," Margaret said. Many young couples and families, like the Robsons, moved into the village, attracted by the idyllic surroundings and the careful forethought that had gone into planning North Palm Beach. The Ross brothers sold lots out of an office in the village hall, according to Christine Schwencke, who worked there one summer.

Charlotte Young Doten, whose father, William "Bill" Young, served North Palm Beach as one of the first elected councilmen, said that her family was the thirty-seventh to move into the village. "The house across the street from us wasn't even finished," she said. "We used to walk to the country club [the Winter Club] from my house. It was just sand. The streets were laid out, but there weren't any houses from Gulf Road or Harbour Road on. Lighthouse Drive wasn't there. There was just sand." The Young family lived on Ebbtide Drive, and Police Chief Dudden lived in a house behind them. "Al Olson, the first village manager, was very nice to us kids," Charlotte said. "There were quite a few [kids] my age there. We'd have a dance at the country club. He used to [also] rent a bus and take us over to the pools in Palm Beach. We'd stay for a few hours and swim and come back, before there was a pool at the country club." The village continued to grow.

Developers Ken May and John Doran, who were also very involved in selling lots in early North Palm Beach, both worked for the Ross brothers when they were in West Palm Beach. May and Doran then shifted their efforts and moved to the village, where they continued selling real estate for the Rosses. Although it was sometimes difficult to gain funding for development projects in the 1950s and 1960s, this was a very lucrative time for both the Rosses and for North Palm Beach Properties. On February 27, 1964, ground was broken for the village post office on U.S. Highway 1. It was completed the same year.

Fred Trapnell, First Utility Manager

Bill Young, North Palm Beach's second village historian, wrote in his history of the town that Fred Trapnell, the first utility manager, had to travel by Jeep, through the sand, to reach a lift station that was part of the sewage system. It was located on the southwest corner of Southwind Drive and Northlake Boulevard. In 1956, the road that is now known as Northlake Boulevard didn't extend east of Prosperity Farms Road.

ALBIN OLSON, FIRST VILLAGE MANAGER

Before the village hall was completed, village manager Albin R. Olson worked in a small room on the upper floor of the Winter Club. In his time as manager, he also served as the treasurer and village clerk. *Village of North Palm Beach.*

North Palm Beach's first village manager, Albin Olson, had a master's degree in public administration from Florida State University. He was also a marine corps veteran who served in World War II and, later, Korea. He once worked as an assistant manager for the town of Port Everglades, and prior to that, he worked in the office of Pensacola's city manager. He'd also worked as an assistant to the city manager in Daytona Beach.

Olson's high level of experience gave the Village of North Palm Beach a solid start, which was just what the town needed. During his time as manager, Olson also served as the village clerk, treasurer, tax collector and assessor. He resigned after seven years, leaving all of these positions in 1963. In a letter to the village council, he stated that he felt his approach to administration had become ineffective.

When Olson first started, he had many responsibilities. Before the village hall was completed, his office operated out of a small room in the upper floor of the Winter Club. There, he handled his first duty: setting up the tax roll. At the time, there were only two taxpayers within the village, North Palm Beach Properties—consisting of the Ross brothers, Jack Schwencke and Jay White—and John MacArthur. Interestingly, there had been a third taxpayer—an absent Frenchman who'd inherited Little Munyon Island but never saw it in person. "When Olson sent him a tax bill, a polite letter came back from France with a check for the taxes due—$23."

Albert Dudden, First Fire and Police Chief

Albert Dudden, who served a few years longer than Olson, was the village's first fire and police chief—later, the director of public safety. Dudden was originally from New York, where he served as a New York State police officer for twenty-nine years. He retired as a police sergeant and moved to Florida, where his family became early residents of the village of North Palm Beach.

Chief Dudden and Officer Ed Henne. Albert Dudden served as chief of police from October 22, 1956, to January 28, 1966. He was the director of public safety—both chief of police and fire chief—for most of his tenure. *Village of North Palm Beach.*

Chief Dudden accepts delivery of the village's very first fire engine. *Village of North Palm Beach.*

Dudden worked for the village alongside Officer Ed Henne, and for a while, the two men made up the entire police force. Before they had a better place to keep the village's first fire truck, it was parked near the country club, where the tennis courts are today. Dudden was the chief at a time when both the fire department and the police were housed in one building. Dudden resigned after nine years due to health issues. By the time he left, he had seven men working with him, but even then, the police force was small.

Architect John L. Volk Designs the Village Hall

The village hall was designed in July 1956, prior to the incorporation of the town, by architect John L. Volk. Volk was born in Austria in 1901. His family came to the United States when he was a child, and Volk grew up in New York City. He studied architecture in Paris and at Columbia University in New York. In the 1920s, when Addison Mizner was at the height of his career, Volk arrived in Florida. He became well known for his designs over the years, even as Mizner's influence began to dwindle.

Architect John L. Volk (*pictured with his wife*) designed the North Palm Beach Village Hall in 1956. *Preservation Foundation of Palm Beach.*

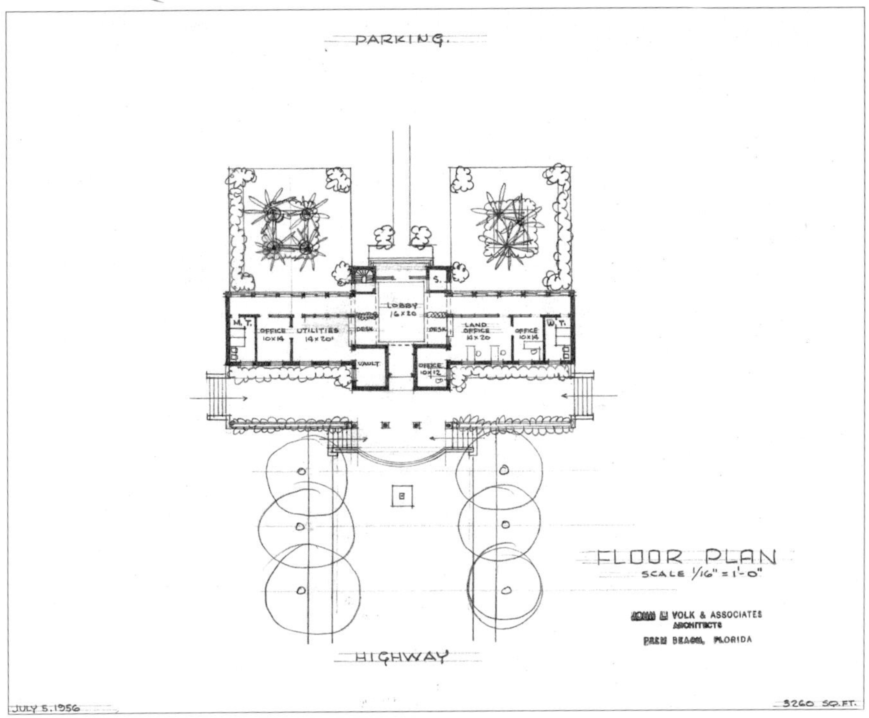

An original sketch of the North Palm Beach Village Hall by John L. Volk. When the village hall was first constructed, North Palm Beach Properties and the Ross brothers sold lots out of an office in the building. *Preservation Foundation of Palm Beach.*

Some of Volk's most memorable buildings were constructed in the late 1930s in West Palm Beach. He not only designed homes for some of Palm Beach's most notable families, including the Pulitzers and Vanderbilts, but his firm was responsible for designing many local public-use buildings. Over the years, his original design for the North Palm Beach Village Hall has remained the same, though additions and improvements have been made to the building.

Village manager Joe J. Eassa, who worked for North Palm Beach from 1966 to 1977, remembered what the village hall looked like before it was renovated. "There were substantial renovations here. We had terrazzo floors in the corridor, the common area," he said. "At one end of the building, we had the entire public safety department. It was included in a relatively small space in the north end of the building." This was before the public safety department was moved to its own building. "My office as village manager was at the other end of the building," Joe added.

Residents pose in front of the village hall after it was built. *Village of North Palm Beach.*

Edwin and Thelma Obert

Among the first families to move into North Palm Beach were the Oberts, Edwin and Thelma. After studying at Dartmouth College and Bellevue Medical College, Dr. Edwin Obert worked as chief of surgical staff at Point Pleasant Hospital and Trenton General Hospital before relocating to Florida. He and his wife moved to North Palm Beach in 1956, and they quickly became active in the fledgling community. Edwin was also a member of the Palm Beach chapter of the Sons of the American Revolution.

Thelma, who was born in New Jersey in 1905, was also college educated and received a master's degree in elementary education supervision from New York University in 1941. When the Oberts moved to North Palm Beach, Thelma became a founding member of the North Palm Beach branch of the American Association of University Women (AAUW), and she later served as the group's president. Thelma's contributions to the founding of the North Palm Beach Public Library also made her an honored village resident.

Dolores Walker Gets Her Day

In 1966, village manager Joe J. Eassa hired Dolores Walker as his secretary. At that time, the position of village clerk was merely a part-time job that paid $600 a year. North Palm Beach was growing at a fast rate, and it soon became clear that the village needed a clerk full-time. Dolores was hired and remained in the position for twenty-four years. She was always remembered as a thoughtful person and a hard worker. According to a *Palm Beach Post* article that was published on December 30, 1990, to honor her retirement, North Palm Beach designated December 28 as "Dolores Walker Day" and "named her office in her honor."

Joe remembered when he hired her, and he recalled the village honoring her contribution in 1990. "Dolores was in the same office [with me as my secretary]," he said. "She became village clerk soon after. She was extraordinary. She came here from Chicago. I hired her as she was working downtown in West Palm Beach. She was proficient and a very fine Christian woman. She did a very good job." After her retirement, Dolores told the *Palm Beach Post*, "Clerks don't know how lucky they are today. Remember the day when they wanted twelve copies of everything, and you had to deal with all that carbon paper?"

North Palm Beach's Relationship to Palm Beach Gardens

John D. MacArthur turned to the west after fighting to exert control over utility operations in Lake Park and selling land to start North Palm Beach. He initially wanted to call his new town "Palm Beach City," but residents of West Palm Beach spoke up against it, claiming the name would've been too confusing. Instead, MacArthur decided to name this new town Palm Beach Gardens. Ground was broken for the town's first buildings in 1958, and it was officially incorporated in 1959. Palm Beach Gardens was solely the work of MacArthur, while Lake Park and North Palm Beach had already exerted their own independence as communities. Although MacArthur had owned much of the land in these towns, the conflict over Lake Park's utilities and the introduction of other players in North Palm Beach's early history may have inspired MacArthur to focus his energies elsewhere. Palm Beach Gardens was uniquely founded by one man with a vision, and for the first five years of its existence, it was run and managed by a council that MacArthur chose himself. After five years had passed, the town's political system switched to one with democratic elections.

Sign of the Times

Segregation was an ongoing issue in the 1950s, and housing policies had yet to be addressed in the United States. The Civil Rights Act wasn't signed until 1964, so tensions between white people and people of color continued to build throughout the 1950s. In 1959, Gaines Construction Company, led by its president, Julius Gaines, announced its plan to build a housing development specifically for well-to-do blacks in North Palm Beach. Intending to build three hundred homes, Gaines purchased ninety-five acres from John D. MacArthur. The houses—some with waterfront property—were meant to overlook the North Palm Beach Country Club and golf course. Prior to this plan, Gaines and Ralph Stolkin had worked to promote properties that MacArthur helped finance in Carol City north of Miami. Despite their professional connections, Gaines told the *Miami News* that MacArthur had absolutely no connection to their new housing development in North Palm Beach.

The village council's reaction to the proposed homes was not only a reflection of the times, but it also hinted at deeper issues in the relationship between MacArthur and the Village of North Palm Beach. While Gaines argued that many black professional people wanted nice homes and could afford to purchase property in the area, Mayor Jay White told the *Miami News*, "MacArthur has told councilmen privately that if he didn't get his oceanfront land out of the town, he would start a Negro development here." The mayor added that he would "fight every effort to start such a project in the village." It is unclear what piece of land the article was referring to, or whether Mayor White simply used an incorrect term when he said "oceanfront." If the term itself is incorrect, it's possible he was referring to MacArthur's 1955 announcement that he would develop subdivisions on Munyon Island. When the village council objected to MacArthur's plan, a lengthy court battle ensued. North Palm Beach refused to give up, and MacArthur's plans were dashed when the U.S. Supreme Court turned down his appeal. Regardless of which piece of land Mayor White was talking about, the fact remains that he suspected MacArthur might be using Gaines's development as a way to get back at the village.

Soon after Gaines's initial announcement, MacArthur stated that he would try to purchase the land back in order to halt the project. He said he had no prior knowledge of Gaines's plans. Today, the story and facts behind this proposed development remain murky. MacArthur's representative and village councilman Charles Cunningham stated, at a council meeting, that he'd been authorized by MacArthur to negotiate the purchase and keep the development from moving forward. The rest remained hearsay, and the dynamic between MacArthur, Gaines and the council became somewhat clouded. However, this dispute remains a good example of the kind of conflicts that surrounded MacArthur, one of the area's most influential landowners.

Northlake Boulevard: A Desolate Stretch

In 1959, the First American Bank became the first building constructed on Northlake Boulevard, which started as a desolate dirt road. At this time, it was considered risky to build anything on this stretch of road, as it wasn't well traveled. There was farmland along Northlake Boulevard west of town, and residents remembered an old farmhouse or shack that sat near present-day Congress Boulevard.

Winship's Prescription Center continues to be the longest-running business in North Palm Beach. It opened in the late 1950s after Robert Winship and his wife, Aileen, moved to the area from New York. The Winships saw a need for a pharmacy in the area, which was growing exponentially due to the arrival of Pratt & Whitney and Radio Corporation of America (RCA). Born in 1928, Robert Winship graduated from Dartmouth College in 1949 and earned his degree in pharmacy from the University of Buffalo. He and Aileen owned Winship's Prescription Center for over twenty years, and he was very active in the North Palm Beach community. He volunteered on many boards, including the Lion's Club and the Knights of Columbus. When the pharmacy opened, it was the only drugstore on Northlake Boulevard.

The second owners of the pharmacy were Linda Paraizo and her husband. Linda began working as an intern pharmacist at Winship's, and she earned her license in 1971. She worked at Winship's Prescription Center until 1975. The couple bought the business from the Winships in 1983 and

Winship's Prescription Center, first opened by Robert and Aileen Winship, has been in business in North Palm Beach for over sixty years. *Author's collection.*

sold it in 2012. "When we sold the pharmacy, we were taking care of the grandchildren of some of those original families," Linda said. She added that, when she returned to Winship's after purchasing the business, she already knew 90 percent of the clients. It is still operating under its original name, and it stands in its second location, on the corner of Northlake Boulevard and Northlake Drive, which was built in 1960 by Robert Winship and Dr. Edward Halder, a dentist. The business was originally located in the area where, as of this book's publication date, the Book Exchange currently stands. The Winships lived on Country Club Drive in North Palm Beach for many years before relocating to Alabama to live with one of their children.

Chapter 6

HOW PRATT & WHITNEY HELPED THE VILLAGE THRIVE

We were the only non-engineers on our street.
—Margaret Robson, North Palm Beach resident

Pratt & Whitney Comes to Town

In 1860, Amos Whitney and Francis Pratt founded Pratt & Whitney in Hartford, Connecticut. The following year, the company started manufacturing guns and related machinery. It wasn't until 1925 that Pratt & Whitney altered its focus and became Pratt & Whitney Aircraft Company. They completed the construction of their first engine—the Wasp—on Christmas Eve 1925, and by March 1926, the United States Navy had ordered two hundred of them.

Northern Palm Beach County still had a lot of empty land and a small population in 1956. Developers began making plans to expand in this area, and with the arrival of Pratt & Whitney—and, later on, RCA—more and more people were attracted to the northern part of the county. Margaret Robson, longtime resident of North Palm Beach, recalled how many of her neighbors were engineers. "There were a lot of engineers from RCA, too," she said. RCA, or Radio Corporation of America, constructed a plant in Palm Beach Gardens in 1960, which also brought jobs to the area and attracted new residents, engineers and their families. RCA considered building this plant in a number of sites around the country before deciding

North Palm Beach grew quickly, in part, because of the Pratt & Whitney plant that was built west of town. This photograph was taken in 1965. *State Library of Florida.*

on Palm Beach County. Subdivisions were built in neighboring towns to cater to the influx of families moving into the area. Most of them were following career opportunities at both Pratt & Whitney and RCA.

John D. MacArthur owned the property where RCA was constructed, and in August 1960, he and Frank Sleeter, the vice president of manufacturing at RCA, signed a contract for the sale of 104 acres. The plant was built on the corner of Monet Road and State Road A1A. By 1973, RCA was the fourth largest employer in Palm Beach County, and at its height, thousands of people worked for the company. However, employment numbers fluctuated as the industry itself changed. Margaret Robson said:

> *The little street* [in North Palm Beach, where] *Norm and I* [moved,] *was almost entirely RCA and Pratt & Whitney engineers.…We were the only non-engineers on the street. A great deal of North Palm Beach was RCA and Pratt & Whitney engineers, and a lot of doctors moved in. It was a little far from Good Samaritan* [Hospital], *but it was a town of professional people.*

An aerial view of the RCA building in Palm Beach Gardens, 1965. *State Library of Florida.*

In the village's infancy, many of its residents worked at the Pratt & Whitney plant, and they brought their families to the area. In 1968, when 1,787 houses were constructed in North Palm Beach, things started to turn around. By that point, a number of people who did not work at Pratt & Whitney also settled in the village. However, the village's early years were certainly shaped by Pratt & Whitney's arrival in Florida.

Claire Hill and her husband were the twentieth or twenty-first family to move to North Palm Beach. As of this writing, Claire resided in an original Ross brothers' home in the village. "My husband worked for Pratt & Whitney in East Hartford, Connecticut," said Claire, who was born in New Hampshire in 1927. Pratt & Whitney recommended that the young couple should move to North Palm Beach. It had become necessary for the company to expand, and they chose South Florida for a specific reason: The type of work they were doing—testing jet engines at night and using liquid hydrogen—required some level of isolation. The area they chose, just west of northern Palm Beach County, provided this type of isolation.

Wendell McEver started working at Pratt & Whitney in 1967, when he was just nineteen years old. Prior to that, he remembered that friends of

Employees check the operation of a machine at the Pratt & Whitney facility, 1959. *State Library of Florida.*

his had worked there, as well as his friends' parents. "We moved to Palm Beach County in 1962. I had friends who worked at Pratt. Some of my friends' dads worked at Pratt and I didn't even know until later on," he said. "Off Prosperity Farms Road, there were a lot of people who worked at Pratt who bought those lots off the Intracoastal [Waterway]." He also said that one of his friends lived on Edgewater Drive.

> [His father] *worked on the assembly floor, and his mother was a chemist with a four-year degree. They built their own house on the water. That's how I ended up at Pratt. I wanted to get ahead in life, and I was always ambitious. My friend's parents said, "Why don't you go to Pratt?" I said, "I don't know anything about that."*
>
> *They told me it was like a city, handed me an application. I drove my old hotrod Dodge out there, and they gave me a job on second shift, moving parts around on the assembly floor. A lot of the people at Pratt who worked second shift either had a side business in the morning or they worked for someone else.*

Wendell added that just about everyone in those days used carpools instead of driving themselves—even if they were supervisors. Wendell went on to serve in the marine corps, and he returned to Pratt with additional

Inside Pratt & Whitney, 1959. *State Library of Florida.*

experience when he left the service. "I was a mechanic then. The plant was actually called the Florida Research and Development Center. Everyone always just called it Pratt."

In 1978, Palm Beach County commissioner Lake Lytal remarked that Pratt & Whitney was largely responsible for turning south Florida into a place where people resided year-round, rather than just a resort destination.

THE CHILDREN REMEMBER

Lisa Huls Humbert, who lived in North Palm Beach as a child before moving with her family to Jupiter Farms, remembered the influence that Pratt & Whitney had on the village. "Our neighborhood was very peaceful. All the kids ran around in the yard and in the streets. A lot of our dads either worked at Pratt & Whitney or RCA," she said. "More [at] Pratt & Whitney." Her own father, Ralph Huls, was an engineer who worked with the company on rockets.

Ray Eberling lived in the North Palm Beach area off and on, beginning in 1959, and both of his parents, at one time, worked for Pratt & Whitney for about a year or two. "My father was an accountant, my mother was a secretary," Ray said. He added that his parents didn't come to Florida with the Pratt & Whitney employees who had arrived from Hartford. Rather, they knew they wanted to live in the area and looked for jobs after they arrived. He said, "I had many, many friends whose fathers—and occasionally mothers—worked [at Pratt & Whitney], some of whom came down with the Hartford move." He remembered Lake Park as a solidly middle-class town and noted, "Since North Palm Beach was pretty much marketed to the Pratt & Whitney families coming down from Hartford, it was a little more upscale. Lake Park was a mix of blue-collar, entry-level [and] white-collar [people], while North Palm Beach was more white-collar."

Susan Tiedemann Bickel, a village councilmember, stated that her father worked for Pratt & Whitney. "As far as I know, all of my friends' dads worked at Pratt," she said. Ann Swiatowski, who grew up in the village, remembered how Pratt & Whitney brought her family to the area. "My dad was an air force fighter pilot. When he got out of the air force, we moved to Florida. We lived on Pelican Way, and my father worked for Pratt & Whitney," she said. "He was a Notre Dame graduate and an aeronautical engineer." She added that, each year, Pratt & Whitney held a fishing contest for its employees on land where, ordinarily, no one was allowed to go. "On this one day, the families could come, and you could go fishing. Some people were catching huge bass, because you couldn't fish there. No one was allowed there except on that day." Many of the children Ann grew up with also had fathers who worked at Pratt & Whitney. "There were picnics, parties, and get-togethers on the beach. Pratt & Whitney provided our family with a very nice life."

Nancy and Alvin Moore

Pratt & Whitney brought Nancy Fant Moore and her husband, Alvin C. Moore, to the fledgling village of North Palm Beach. "My husband was in the navy for ten years," Nancy said. "He was in the invasion of Normandy." After Alvin left the service, Nancy recalled that he didn't have enough skills to put to good use, so "he decided he'd better go back to college." She continued, "He graduated in 1957. He was interviewed by United Technologies, and they didn't have a plant in Florida then, but we knew we wanted to come back to Florida. He had been in the navy, stationed in Jacksonville, and we liked it there." The company agreed to relocate them to Florida, but only after they moved to Hartford, Connecticut, first. "We went there in 1957. Then, in 1958, we came back down here. We were there for a year. We have lived here ever since."

The Moores first moved to Lake Park, because there wasn't much in North Palm Beach at the time. They eventually wanted more space between their home and their neighbors' houses, and they finally found what they were looking for in North Palm Beach. "We moved to North Palm Beach, and I wouldn't want to live in any other place. It truly is the best place to live under the sun, and that's just the way I feel. There are wonderful people in North Palm, and it's home to me." A number of North Palm Beach's early councilmembers were Pratt & Whitney personnel, including Alvin, who also served as mayor. Additionally, he served on the North Palm Beach Planning and Zoning Advisory Board.

SHIFTING TIMES

Pratt & Whitney remained a fixture in the area. However, as the electronics and manufacturing industries changed over the years, production at the Palm Beach Gardens RCA plant began to decline. The plant laid off a number of its employees in 1980 and 1981, and the plant's main product—semiconductors—were no longer in high demand. In 1985, it was announced the RCA plant would close. Hundreds of people lost their jobs.

Chapter 7

THE HEART OF FLORIDA'S GOLD COAST

I remember the dairy on Northlake. I remember fields. What I remember more [than anything] *is everything being sandy and having a ton of little friends in the neighborhood to play with.*
—Susan Tiedemann Bickel, North Palm Beach councilmember

AN IDYLLIC CHILDHOOD

Children who grew up in the village remembered playing outdoors, knowing everyone in their neighborhood and biking to Juno Beach. When Ann Swiatowski was fifteen years old, she bought a horse with her best friend, and they kept it in a stable near Military Trail. They often rode east along Northlake. "There was a pizza place there, a convenience store, and we would hop on a horse and ride to the store," she said. "Occasionally, we would ride all the way to Juno Beach."

Ann was born in 1960 and remembered her idyllic childhood in North Palm Beach. "It was safe. Everyone knew everyone else." Her parents were originally from the Chicago area, and her father didn't want his kids to grow up in that kind of weather. Ann recalled, "He said, 'My kids are going to grow up where there's sunshine and they can play outside year-round and the weather is nice.'" She added that her father felt the sunsets in South Florida couldn't be beat.

> *There were lakes* [out west], *which is now PGA National. We took our horses there and went swimming and hung out for the day. I had a friend who lived way out west on Northlake, where there were just a couple*

> *of houses and an alligator farm. We rode our horses around there.* [My friend] *had a little motor bike. I wouldn't trade my childhood for anything.*

A CAREFREE LIFE

Before Northlake Boulevard was developed, some farmland still remained there, and the children who grew up in North Palm Beach in the early 1960s and 1970s remembered watching the last vestiges of this unspoiled paradise disappear as more businesses and developments came to the area. Susan Tiedemann Bickel recalled the details of her parents' first house before they moved to North Palm Beach—a tiny little place on the beach in Juno. When she was a child, her family frequented the beach there; it was empty of buildings, sidewalks and paths at the time. "You could look down the dune to see where other people had gone so you wouldn't get sand burrs on you," she said, and she added that they made their own paths to the surf.

Ann Swiatowski said that she and her friends would wake each other up early in the morning—sometimes at 3:00 a.m.—to go fishing.

> *We went on foot to the lagoon. The lagoon backs up to Prosperity Farms Road now, and it's all built-up, but that was one of our hangouts. There was a tree that had a big rope. We would leave early in the morning. My mom wouldn't even be up yet. Sometimes we went home for lunch, sometimes we brought peanut butter and jelly sandwiches, and we'd come home for dinner. We'd be there all day long.*

Christine Schwencke said that there were often parties at private homes and that everything in North Palm Beach revolved around sports and school activities. "My brothers played golf at the country club, and my sister did a lot of horseback riding." She added, "It was just a great place to grow up. There was lots to do: the beach, sports, tennis, golf, horseback riding and there seemed to be a wide variety of people to grow up with who were very interesting, and we were all a close-knit group and still are."

AN EXPANDING COMMUNITY

In the mid-1950s, the council began to consider purchasing both the village hall and the country club. Part of the decision regarding the country club was based on the possibility that the club and surrounding lands could be subject to development if it wasn't owned by the village. But at the time of the council's first discussions, it still didn't know how much the property would cost. North Palm Beach Properties Inc. had yet to name a price, and this process alone took some time.

The council then agreed to purchase the village hall in 1958 for $206,213—the same amount that the developers spent to build it. Additionally, village manager Albin Olson was given the go-ahead to work out an agreement with Lake Park "for exchange of fire and police protection in emergencies," since North Palm Beach's public safety department was still very small.

Parks and Recreation

Dick Ross served as the town's second mayor in 1957. In the same year, the Ross brothers donated land to the village to build Anchorage Park. They also donated land for North Palm Beach Marina, which was completed in 1963. The following year, the village council discussed creating a bond legislation to set up a recreation project. According to the *Palm Beach Post*, "The measure authorizes the expenditure of $1,015,000 for purchase of the North Palm Beach Country Club and $415,000 for creation of a swimming pool and related facilities." The village's residents feared that their taxes would go up, and they were worried these projects wouldn't make enough money to recoup the costs of purchasing the country club property and building the pool. Part of the council's plans for the country club included building tennis courts, boat ramps and shuffleboard courts, along with baseball fields and an area for senior citizens, which also increased residents' concerns.

Mayor Thomas and the council weren't worried; they felt that the projects would make enough money to cover all of the costs. In 1963, the village completed the new country club building, which was located next to the old Winter Club. According to a *Palm Beach Post* announcement from December 25, 1963, a free dance party was held on the opening night of the new country club building. The announcement also stated, "Village manager Albin R. Olson said the party will be limited to community residents and country club members. A formal opening of a new swimming pool and eighteen-hole golf course will be held later." Steve Higgins recalled that his father, Norman Higgins of Higgins Plastering Company, completed the plastering and other related work on the pool when it was installed. It was completed around the fall of 1962.

North Palm Beach Marina, 2019. *Author's collection.*

The country club under construction in 1962. The Winter Club stood beside it. *Village of North Palm Beach.*

This image shows the close proximity of the Winter Club to the 1963 club and swimming pool. *Village of North Palm Beach.*

Village historian Bill Young wrote in his official history for the village's twenty-fifth anniversary that Osborne Park started out as "a sandy lot with a tall television tower in its center, owned by Channel 5." When the company decided to relocate, the council bought the land and developed Osborne Park. Evidence of the transmitting station still exists next door at the First Presbyterian Church of North Palm Beach.

Lakeside Park was developed from a strip of land along Lake Worth, located at the end of Lighthouse Drive. Shuffleboard courts were constructed next to the library in 1961. In 1980, village resident George Delacorte donated funds to help build a new community center on Prosperity Farms Road. The eighteen-hole golf course remains the central pride and joy of the village.

North Palm Beach Champions

Professional golfer Bob Hayes joined the staff of the new country club, along with dining room manager Marcel Berthault, golf course superintendent Sid

Alma Beck getting ready to go diving in Palm Beach Shores inlet in 1952. *Robin Murphy*.

Clarke and pool manager Alma Beck, who was a national AAU underwater spearfishing women's champion in 1959. Beck was also the co-holder of the state championship title in 1960 and 1961 and a model. Charlotte Young Doten remembered Alma.

> *The pool* [at the country club] *was finished before the new building was. We all had memberships, and I worked at the pool one summer. I was a lifeguard, but I was mainly in the check-in room, where you signed in. Alma oversaw the lifeguards. She was a lot of fun. She was a free spirit, and she had a wonderful kindergarten on Singer Island.*

Robin Murphy, Alma's niece, remembered her aunt with fondness. "She ran Singer Shores Kindergarten. She was my favorite aunt." Swimming lessons were also included for children at the kindergarten.

Left: The opening ceremony for the new country club was held in 1963. *Village of North Palm Beach.*

Below: Richard Cavanah and his crew painting the pool at the country club. *Richard Cavanah.*

The pool at the North Palm Beach Country Club in 1980. *Richard Cavanah.*

Richard Cavanah joined the village's country club as swim coach in 1975. He remembered how closely together the two buildings were situated. Prior to Richard's tenure, Buddy Baarcke managed the pool. "I have a lot of fond memories here," Richard said. When he took over, he began painting the pool every two years. "It's like my second home. I love it. All the palm trees that were here [around the pool], I grew them from coconuts and brought them up here and planted them. They just took them out. They were right in front of the pool snack bar."

Richard said that the club's swim program is one of the best and oldest in South Florida. "We've had hundreds of kids who went off to swim in college and get scholarships." In 1992, when Ryan Berube was a senior in high school, Richard took him to the Olympic trials. "Only a handful of high school kids go to the trials. He did so well there, I knew he would make the Olympic team one day if he was still swimming. Sure enough, he did." Laura Bennett Reback was another North Palm Beach success story, and she went on to become a professional triathlete. Richard added, "We've had countless numbers of kids go to the national championships, junior national championships, and state high school champions for swimming."

The Mayor's Daughter

Walter E. Thomas served as the mayor of North Palm Beach from 1960 to 1961. Pam Thomas Wagner witnessed the early days of the village and fondly recalled what it was like to be the mayor's daughter.

> *Even though we lived in many places, all of my brothers and I consider North Palm Beach to be home. My oldest brother remembers taking off on his bike early in the morning to go to fishing in the ocean all day with a friend. And those mosquito trucks…what fun, riding our bikes behind them and mooching kumquats from neighbors' trees along the way. My sweetest memory was going house to house to campaign for my father. I was so proud to be the mayor's daughter.*

Pam was a resident of North Palm Beach from 1957 to 1964. The Thomas family was the fifty-fifth family to move to the village.

Always Planning for the Future

As the village grew, the council stayed true to the plans that were initially set forth by the founders. Thomas F. Lewis became mayor in 1965 and served the village until 1970. Lewis was drawn to North Palm Beach because of his position with Pratt & Whitney. As a former gunner in the air force, he had become a project manager for the company's jet and rocket engine program.

During his first year as mayor, Lewis sought to reexamine the village's original plans, with the idea of attracting more commerce. He felt the village needed more income, so he suggested a five-year plan for development. According to the *Palm Beach Post*, "North Palm Beach wasn't doing too well, and Lewis, a political unknown, ran for a town council seat. He won, became mayor and played a major role in helping the town right itself." North Palm Beach Properties' and the Ross brothers' original plans for the village involved maintaining a higher-end atmosphere on U.S. Highway 1 through North Palm Beach. Even as Mayor Lewis and the council took a closer look at revitalizing the village's five-year plan, this original concept was maintained.

Mayor Thomas F. Lewis presiding over the grand opening of the North Palm Beach Public Library building on Anchorage Drive in 1969. He went on to become a congressman. *Village of North Palm Beach.*

THEODORE PRATT SPEAKS AT TENCENNIAL CELEBRATION

In January 1967, a celebration was held in honor of North Palm Beach's first families and to commemorate the tenth anniversary of the village's founding. While the actual tenth anniversary of North Palm Beach's founding was October 24, 1966, the celebration took place on January 13, 14 and 15, 1967. At 8:00 a.m. on Friday, January 13, church bells rang and sirens went off for a total of three minutes. The "tencennial" celebration included a boat and car show in the parking lot of the First American Bank and a parade that began at 10:00 a.m. The local high school's band played a concert at 11:00 a.m. At noon, Mayor Lewis presided over a pioneer luncheon, where Theodore Pratt, a well-known author of Floridian nonfiction and fiction, including *The Barefoot Mailman*, was the guest speaker. A busy afternoon followed, which included golf matches, swimming, a surfing contest and a book fair and open house at the library. A cocktail party and an award dinner ended the illustrious evening.

Chapter 8

SOCIAL LIFE IN THE VILLAGE

I joined the Junior Woman's Club. I was young then, and that's how you would get acquainted with people.
—Nancy Moore, first official director of the North Palm Beach Public Library

THE JUNIOR WOMAN'S CLUB

Clubs have always been a popular way to get involved and make friends in the North Palm Beach community, and women's clubs were especially important to the town's social scene in the 1950s. Women's clubs served their communities in a variety of ways, which included supporting education and creating libraries. The Junior Woman's Club of North Palm Beach was mostly made up of young married women.

On June 3, 1961, the Florida Federation of Women's Clubs convention was held at the Barcelona Hotel in Miami Beach. There, the Junior Woman's Club of North Palm Beach was given five awards, including awards in the categories of junior education, home life, fine arts and budgeting. According to the *Palm Beach Post*, the women who represented the club at the convention included "Mrs. James Roberson, president; Mrs. John V. Wible, immediate past president; Mrs. Douglas G. Howell; Mrs. Philip Richards; Mrs. Keith M. Nichols; Mrs. Frederick Engel; Mrs. Lloyd D. Flood; Mrs. Howard Cook Jr.; and Mrs. Robert C. Woolfe."

The club's members also won their own awards. In 1967, the North Palm Beach branch named Arlette Griner "Woman of the Year." She'd donated

In its heyday, the Winter Club was the center of North Palm Beach's social scene. This photograph shows a Christmas party that took place on the back patio on December 21, 1957. *Photographer Sam R. Quincey. Village of North Palm Beach.*

her time as an editor for the club's monthly newsletter, and she headed a U.S. Savings Stamp sales program at the elementary school. She was also the chairwoman for the club's rummage sale and summer auction. The club held an annual fashion show, and Arlette was one of the models. To top it all off, she served the Junior Woman's Club as their historian.

North Palm Beach Lions Club

Like North Palm Beach's women, who had their own clubs, the men had clubs of their own. In the 1950s and 1960s, Lions Club International had yet to admit women into its ranks. Much like women's clubs, the Lions Club was focused mainly on raising money for its worthy causes. Edwin J. Obert was an early member of the North Palm Beach Lions Club, and he served

In 1960, Albin Olson (*center*) was appointed as the president of the North Palm Beach Lions Club. Here, Robert Cromwell is pictured passing him the gavel. Edwin Obert (*right*) was the first president of the club. *Village of North Palm Beach.*

as its first president. On April 8, 1964, he was the evening speaker at the club's meeting, which was held at the North Palm Beach Country Club. During his speech, he lectured the club's members on a round-the-world trip he'd taken. In March 1960, Mayor Jay H. White was a lecturer at the Lions Club's dinner meeting. An article about the meeting in the paper read, "J.H. White, mayor of North Palm Beach, will speak and show movies of his recent African hunting trip."

While raising money for charity remained an important goal for the group, it also focused on socializing its members and sharing experiences. The North Palm Beach Lions Club members participated in a county-wide "light bulb sale" in October 1960. After selling thousands of bags of light bulbs the year before—for the same promotion—the club collected $50,000 in profit, which went to the Sight Conservation Fund to help provide needy children with eye examinations and glasses.

The clubs in North Palm Beach, as in many towns, were great sources of friendship and connection for residents. They also provided a way for community members to rally and help others, both inside and outside the town.

Garden Club

In February 1959, an advertisement in the *Palm Beach Post* called North Palm Beach "a community of fine homes and beautiful gardens." The article in the advertisement discusses the creation of garden clubs and how they are meant to help facilitate the continued beautification of a town. "It didn't take the residents of the village long to organize their own North Palm Beach Garden Club, with a firm constitution and by-laws which 'mean business' in every sense of the word." Members were expected to be active; if a member missed three meetings in a row, their membership was revoked. "The club meets on the second Wednesday of each month, from October through June, at the North Palm Beach Country Club, with members of the executive board meeting on the first Wednesday of every month." When the article was published, the group had been in existence for less than a year.

On March 16, 1962, the club hosted a "Mad Hatters" luncheon and fashion show to fund the beautification of the village. All the proceeds went to improving the west side of U.S. Highway 1. The ladies took part in a fashion show that awarded prizes for "most beautiful hat," "craziest hat" and "most unusual hat." The Garden Club was also involved in the push to get North Palm Beach named as an official bird sanctuary in 1968. However, newspaper archives don't seem to note the group's existence after 1994.

THE NORTH PALM BEACH YACHT CLUB

Yacht Club Drive in North Palm Beach is named after a clubhouse that was almost built but never came to fruition. For whatever reason, the developers weren't able to gain the interest or the funding to actually build the clubhouse. Joseph A. Tringali, who was on the village council for six years and served as the mayor for one term in 2000, is also the historian of the North Palm Beach Yacht Club. Prior to his work in local politics, he was an assistant district attorney in Buffalo, New York; he then came to Florida and worked as a trial prosecutor. In 1976, Joe and his wife, Mary Lou, moved back to New York to raise their children. In 1990, the couple returned to Florida. "I spent the rest of my career as an assistant attorney general doing appellate law cases," Joe said.

When they moved back to the village in the 1990s, Joe looked for a yacht club to join. He found a group charter from the 1950s and a fledgling club—which mainly consisted of winter residents—that operated out of the marina. The original club had a blue burgee, or triangular flag, with a blue background and a club crest with "NPB" written in white. "The club was supposed to be on Yacht Club Drive, but they never built it," he said, adding that it was intended to be near the marina. "The idea was if you bought a home in North Palm Beach, you would automatically be a member of the Yacht Club. It never happened."

The club dissolved once after its initial founding, but it reemerged in 1975, when Edwin F. Schwarzer—then-owner of the North Palm Beach Marina—joined with his brother, Fred, to reignite interest, and the North Palm Beach Cruise and Yacht Club was incorporated as a nonprofit. Robert Unger designed a new blue and gold burgee with a white "N," and Ed Schwarzer became the first club commodore. Other founding members included Henry VanNimwegen and Jack Folk. For a third time, in 1988, the club had nowhere to go and started to dissolve when the marina was sold to Old Port Cove Holdings.

When Joe tried to revitalize the yacht club in the 1990s, he located the group, attended a meeting and started making suggestions. He was soon elected commodore and joined forces with Jim Peterson, another member of the club, to help bring it back to life. In 1997, the club designed a new burgee that combined elements from the last two designs. In the same year, Mark Hodgkins, the head of the Village of North Palm Beach Recreation Department, called Joe and asked if the Yacht Club had a singing group. At a moment's notice, Joe formed a men's glee club out of the North Palm

The first performance of the North Palm Beach Yacht Club Glee Club at the Village of North Palm Beach's tree-lighting ceremony. *Joseph A. Tringali.*

Visitors were welcome at potluck parties hosted by the North Palm Beach Yacht Club at the Herb Watt building. *Joseph A. Tringali.*

Beach Yacht Club, and they performed at the annual North Palm Beach tree-lighting ceremony. The group also began publishing a monthly newsletter called *The Ship's Wheel*, and in 1998, the club was once again registered with the Yachting Club of America. The club also joined the International Order of the Blue Gavel, the association of yacht club commodores.

The club was eventually moved into the Herb Watt building—which once stood beside the library on Anchorage Drive—after the North Palm Beach Recreation Department moved from there to a new building. "We needed a place to meet," Joe said, adding that the Herb Watt building had to be fixed up a bit first. "A lot of different groups were using it as a meeting place. We arranged to go in and make it habitable. We scheduled meetings for the fourth Monday of every month." The group painted the inside of the building and decorated it with a nautical theme. They held potluck dinners and welcomed visitors there. Despite the difficulties the club had in finding a meeting place, its members remained steadfast and stuck together. With such a water-centered community, having a yacht club and keeping it going simply made sense.

Always Outdoors

Golf has always been a big part of life in North Palm Beach. Christine Schwencke remembered how important golf and boating were to the families who lived in the village. The Schwencke family knew some of the early North Palm Beach professionals, including Frank Shuster, whose son, David, also became an avid golfer. "[The Ross brothers] had to redesign the golf course when they bought it," Christine said of the brothers' initial land purchase. "It was quite rough. They redid the whole driving range." Christine said that her brothers were very good junior golfers, or golfers between the ages of thirteen and eighteen. "I took them to a lot of tournaments all around the state of Florida. North Palm Beach produced a lot of really good junior golfers who went on to play golf for the rest of their lives."

Many residents owned boats, enjoyed the water and went fishing on weekends. Christine remembered how people got together and spent time

Until the village published a more widely circulated newsletter, *Forecast: The North Palm Beach Country Club Magazine* kept its readers apprised of club members' accomplishments and news about swimming, golf, tennis and other events. *Richard Cavanah.*

outdoors. Her father, Jack Schwencke, coached Little League baseball and was remembered fondly by the children of the village. Steve Higgins, whose family moved to the village in 1958, recalled playing for the Pony League as a kid. "Coach Schwencke built us a baseball field so we could play Pony League baseball," Steve said. On Thursday, July 27, 1961, the team was getting ready to meet Boynton Beach and play for the sub-district title. Steve was one of the players on this team. In 1962, Schwencke's team had a perfect record and won the county championship.

Chapter 9

BUILDING A SPIRITUAL PRACTICE

I saw an ad in the paper…about the Unitarian church. They had a good-sized crowd there. The people sponsoring it were the Ross brothers [Dick and Bob].
—Margaret Robson, North Palm Beach resident

Coming Together in Faith

The churches and spiritual practices of the village reflect the various religious backgrounds of its citizens. Margaret Robson, who was born in Daytona Beach in 1928, married architect Norman Robson in 1953. The Robsons were some of the original founders of the Unitarian congregation in North Palm Beach. Margaret recalled learning about Unitarianism in college. She said that when she and Norman began dating, they had not yet decided which religious path they would take together, but one day, she saw an advertisement in the paper for a Unitarian gathering in West Palm Beach. "I said to my husband, who I was just dating at the time, 'I heard about that. Let's go.'" Margaret said, "We went, and it was very interesting. They had a good-sized crowd there. The people sponsoring it were the Ross [brothers, Dick and Bob]." Dick Ross and his wife, Marie, and Bob Ross and his wife, Edie, along with their good friends, the Blakeslees, all had small children. "They wanted a liberal religious education for their children," Margaret recalled. "That's what they were trying to start. They told people they would begin holding Sunday discussion groups, and they did, and Norm and I started going." The Robsons were married soon after, and they later joined the Unitarian congregation.

The founders of the Unitarian church in West Palm Beach, including the Rosses, began gathering in 1952. Margaret said that the Robsons were among the first twenty people to join the fellowship. "It wasn't long before we had forty people. [The Rosses and Blakeslees] wrote to the headquarters in Boston and bought the workbooks, and they were holding Sunday morning religious education programs in their own homes." Soon, Margaret added, there was a crowd of children in the congregation. The group began meeting at the Alfar Dairy Club House in West Palm Beach.

> [Norm and I] *weren't married there. We were married at the First Methodist church where my grandparents belonged, but we almost immediately joined the Unitarian group and went to their meetings, and as soon as they got enough members—and it grew quickly—they leased or rented an empty Greek Orthodox church that was available, just north of Good Samaritan Hospital, a couple blocks off Flagler Drive.*

The congregation continued to grow and attracted some wealthy people who were able to help fund the efforts. In 1963, the group obtained official status as a church, and their first minister was Reverend Dr. William J. Arms. He served in this position from 1958 to 1962. After that, Reverend Jack Loadman served from 1962 to 1967; Reverend John Rose; Reverend Dr. Waldemar Argow from 1974 to 1980; Reverend Dr. Ralph N. Helverson from 1981 to 1989; interim minister Reverend Dr. Janet Newman from 1989 to 1990; and, most recently, Reverend Roger Cowan.

In the same year that the congregation officially became a church, in 1963, they moved into a building in West Palm Beach, which Margaret's husband, Norman, then refurbished. "We met there for a number of years before the congregation decided [it was time to move]," Margaret said. "The hot area was North Palm Beach." In 1987, the church relocated to their current location in North Palm Beach on Prosperity Farms Road. Though other churches had been founded in North Palm Beach prior to the arrival of the Unitarian church, and although the Ross brothers were no longer involved in the church by the time it moved to the village, it is important to note the connection between the local Unitarian church and Dick and Bob Ross, who developed North Palm Beach.

A few years later, on December 7, 1990, Richard "Dick" Ross passed away in Wisconsin at his daughter's home. Although he'd left Florida and had been living in New York City, he was remembered as a "driving force" behind the development of the village. Certainly, he and his brother had a great impact on the founding of the local Unitarian church and its subsequent move.

Faith Lutheran Church

As the first church in North Palm Beach, Faith Lutheran purchased their building on the corner of Ebbtide and U.S. 1 in 1958 for $33,000. According to the church's website and its individual history, fifty-four members signed the church's charter on December 7, 1958. The groundbreaking for the building took place on December 18, 1960, and the church was dedicated on May 14, 1961.

St. Clare Catholic Church

One of the first congregations in North Palm Beach was St. Clare Catholic Church—though they didn't have an actual building until 1969. The group began in Riviera Beach in 1958 as a mission from St. Francis of Assisi Church, and the congregation was established in 1960. Reverend Joseph McLaughlin became the church's first pastor. Initially, they met wherever they could, including in a shopping center and in congregants' homes. In 1961, the church purchased land on Prosperity Farms Road. There was already a small house on the property, which later became the parish office. The church began raising funds to build a school. On July 27, 1963, ground was broken for the building, and construction was completed in late December, just before Christmas. The school opened in September 1964, and it provided Catholic education for local children.

The St. Clare Catholic School grew and expanded, adding grades and classroom space in 1967. Ed Lucas spearheaded the campaign to raise additional funds, and the rectory was constructed at the cost of $18,000. The church also purchased three buses for the school. A church building that could hold one thousand people was constructed near the school in 1968 and the first eight months of 1969. The building was dedicated on September 13, 1969.

In the small, tight-knit neighborhood of North Palm Beach, Ann Swiatowski could walk to the St. Clare Catholic School. "We were Catholic, and we went to St. Clare's for church. We [also] went to school there. My mom had looked at property off PGA, and she said, 'Why would anyone want to live here? There's nothing over here.' At the time, there wasn't." Ann attended St. Clare's from first through eighth grade. She remembered the house where the priests resided nearby. "It was just a [church] community within our little street. The only kids I knew growing up went to St. Clare's," she said. "All of my friends and neighbors [were] people we knew from church. It was really tight-knit. Everyone knew everyone." The parish hall that is currently in use today was constructed in 1977. A library was also added to the church in 1978, and the St. Clare Catholic School was accredited by the Florida Catholic Conference in 1979. A new library building was completed in 1986.

LIGHTHOUSE BAPTIST CHURCH

Lighthouse Baptist Church was started as a mission while the church continued to search for its first building in February 1961. The mission held its first services on April 2, 1961, in a member's home. It later held its first services as a full-fledged congregation in a new church building on Easter Sunday in 1962, according to the *Palm Beach Post*. Theodore Burrell became the church's first pastor. Other church officers included deacons Les Harrell, Jim Lee, Carl Gibbs, Mark Summers, Robert Mutz, Carey Bussell, Roy Nance and Jack Hallman.

THE FIRST PRESBYTERIAN CHURCH OF NORTH PALM BEACH

During the Presbyterian General Assembly of 1861, the church split into two factions—north and south—due to the differing political and theological opinions of either side at the beginning of the Civil War. The Presbyterian Church of the United States (Southern) and the Presbyterian Church in the United States of America (Northern) both had congregations in Palm Beach County.

Families heading into church at the First Presbyterian Church of North Palm Beach, circa the mid-1960s. *First Presbyterian Church of North Palm Beach.*

Much of the Presbyterian presence in Palm Beach County can be credited to the work of Dr. Ryan Lee Wood, a Southern Presbyterian who served as the pastor of Memorial Presbyterian Church on Olive Avenue in West Palm Beach for twenty-five years. As the Palm Beach County and Treasure Coast areas grew and witnessed further development in the 1950s, Dr. Wood felt there should be more Southern Presbyterian churches to serve the expanding communities.

Walter B. "Lucky" Arnold III, the senior pastor of First Presbyterian Church in North Palm Beach, stated that Dr. Wood began an initiative to plant churches in the Central and South Florida areas. Supported by the energy and enthusiasm of his congregation at Memorial Presbyterian, Dr. Wood encouraged outreach, not just in Palm Beach County, but throughout the world, and he encouraged people to build church locations and spread the word of the Presbyterian church. Ed Elliott, a football player for the University of Richmond, became a protégé of Dr. Wood, who helped him find work and become a banker. Elliott also became one of the church's first elders. "I think Dr. Wood's relationship with Ed was an impetus to launching this church," Reverend Arnold said. The idea for the church was formed, and they began meeting around 1962 at the Port of Palm Beach. Once the church had seventy-five members, the fledgling group began thinking about finding a permanent location for a new church. At that time, John D. MacArthur had begun selling off the land he owned in northern Palm Beach

A transmitting tower once stood on this platform. According to historian Bill Young, it was once owned by Channel 5. It still sits on the property of the First Presbyterian Church of North Palm Beach, next to Osborne Park. *Author's collection.*

County, and the church bought land from the village in 1963. The village kept part of the lot and built Osborne Park next to the church property.

Hawkins Hall, a structure that remains on the church property today, is part of the original transmitting station which village historian Bill Young stated in his official village history was once owned by Channel 5, and it was the first building the church used for all of its services. The church added onto the building. However, the back of the structure, which still has a flat roof, is the original part of the building that was used as the radio transmitting station. The part of the building that has a pitched roof and a wooden ceiling was constructed by the church. One of the concrete anchors that was used for the radio tower got in the way when workers began constructing a new two-story Christian education building on another part of the church property. Despite digging deep with jackhammers, the workers were unable to get to the bottom of the triangular concrete block, so they decided to build the foundation over it. Years later, because of the obstruction underneath, the walkway, which was attached to a column, began separating, as the column had settled differently than the rest of the building. An architect had to be called in to repair the problem.

In 1968, when James F. Anderson was the pastor of First Presbyterian, the church built a new chapel and Sunday school building. This new building provided an office space for the pastor and a new secretary space. "And then we built a sanctuary, which is our chapel now," Reverend Arnold said. "That was our sanctuary when I arrived. I came and joined the staff as the associate pastor." The senior pastor at the time was James Stout.

A year and a day after Arnold arrived, Stout left, and the church started what turned out to be a two-year-long search for its next senior pastor. Joanna Hogan, one of the church's original founding members, was on the search committee. When they finally found someone, things didn't work out. Around the same time, the Northern and Southern Presbyterian Churches—which were divided during the Civil War—decided to remerge. For a short time, a rule that kept associate pastors from becoming a church's next senior pastor was waived, so First Presbyterian's committee decided

The flat-roofed portion of Hawkins Hall is part of the original transmitting station. The front of the building was an addition. *Author's collection.*

The groundbreaking for the church's sanctuary. Reverend Arnold (*left*) is standing in front, holding a shovel. *First Presbyterian Church of North Palm Beach.*

The First Presbyterian Church sanctuary in North Palm Beach, built in the 1980s. *First Presbyterian Church of North Palm Beach.*

that they wanted Lucky Arnold to be the church's next pastor. In 1983, Reverend Arnold stepped into the position and has been the church's senior pastor ever since. "We built the sanctuary in about 1984 and 1985," he said. Other buildings were added in the 1990s and early 2000s. "We feel like we're the keeper of Dr. Ryan Wood's flame," Reverend Arnold said. "We have tried to [continue the tradition], to plant churches and launch people into ministry. That's a tribute to Dr. Wood."

Our Lady of Florida Passionist Retreat

In June 1962, Our Lady of Florida Passionist Retreat—which was Catholic and belonged to the Congregation of Passion—was dedicated as a monastery and retreat house. After the retreat had difficulty raising funds, it was closed in 1989. But it reopened in 1992, with the help of the Diocese of Palm Beach.

Chapter 10

PUBLIC AND PRIVATE EDUCATION

We moved to North Palm Beach on Labor Day in 1958, because a new school—North Palm Beach Elementary—was opening. After thirty-six wonderful years of teaching there, I retired in 1994.
—Jeanne Saunders, North Palm Beach resident and educator

North Palm Beach Elementary School

Before a school was constructed in North Palm Beach, the village's children took the bus to schools in Lake Park. The groundbreaking for North Palm Beach Elementary took place on February 19, 1958. The Ross brothers of North Palm Beach Properties Inc.—along with Jack Schwencke and Jay H. White—donated ten acres of land for the school. The building cost $285,000. The people who attended the groundbreaking included Robert R. Horner of the board of public instruction; Mayor Richard Ross and his brother Bob Ross; Jack Schwencke; BPI vice-chairman Ralph Kettler; Elizabeth Hand of BPI; BPI chairman Henry Earwood; BPI architect Edgar S. Wortman; Howell L. Watkins, superintendent of schools; vice-mayor Jay H. White; Councilman Charles Cunningham; and village manager Albin Olson.

Henrietta Jeanne Saunders, a close friend of Nancy Moore, was soon working at the school as a teacher. Jeanne, who was born in 1926 at Good Samaritan Hospital in West Palm Beach, taught at the elementary school for thirty-six years. She recalled the social dances—led by Alma Beck—which were held on Fridays during the school's first ten years

The groundbreaking for North Palm Beach Elementary School on February 19, 1958. Dick Ross (*right*) is standing in front, wearing a jacket and a white sweater vest. His brother, Bob, is behind him, on the right. On the far right side of the photo, next to Bob, is Jack Schwencke, who is pictured wearing a dark suit. *Village of North Palm Beach.*

of operation. After Saunders retired from teaching in 1999, she began working at the North Palm Beach Public Library across the street. She started working in the children's department, but she later moved to reference, where she processed interlibrary loans.

THE BENJAMIN SCHOOL

For the parents of North Palm Beach who sought a private school education for their gifted children, there was the North Palm Beach Private School, which later became the Benjamin School. Initially, the school was started because the village needed a preschool and kindergarten. The school opened in 1960, with a total of seventeen students. Claire Hill substituted at North Palm Beach Private School, and she said, "Nancy and Marshall Benjamin went to our church [the Unitarian Church in West Palm Beach], and we were good friends with them." She added, "That's how I got started with them. My daughter used to babysit the Benjamins' children. They were great educators."

Margaret Robson—who was an educator herself—and her husband witnessed the formation of this school through their friendship with the Rosses. One day, Margaret said, Bob Ross and his wife, Edie, called her and invited her to dinner. They had met a couple whom they hoped would start a school in North Palm Beach, and they wanted Margaret to attend dinner and discuss education with them. Because the village was attracting engineers and other professionals, the Rosses felt that a school was needed for these families—especially a preschool and a kindergarten. Margaret recalled that the couple was very nice. The Rosses sold them a little house on McLaren Road to start a preschool.

In 1961, the school's classes were limited to twenty students, and the school had eighty students—all preschool and kindergarten age—overall. One of the school's first teachers was Jane Rankine, who taught preschool and had twenty-five years of experience as a teacher. She graduated from Eastern Michigan University. An article in an October 1961 edition of the *Palm Beach Post* stated, "Mrs. Benjamin said that the school will offer first grade instruction in 1962 and will add one additional grade each year until it has classes up to and including grade six." The president of the school's board of trustees, developer Llwyd Ecclestone, was one of several who worked to persuade Marshall Benjamin to add grades. Marshall's focus was quality education, not any kind of notoriety, so it also took some convincing before the school changed its name to the Benjamin School.

Before more education was provided closer to the village, many children were bused across town and out of the area. North Palm Beach's parents wanted a good education for their kids, one that was closer to home and didn't require such a long commute. Christine Schwencke attended Riviera Beach High School—class of 1962—at a time when all of the kids from Singer Island, Lake Park and North Palm Beach went to the same high school. Despite the fact that many people moved away over the years, Christine said, "We have high school reunions every five years, and we come from all over the country to be together."

Jane Higginbotham, who taught at the Benjamin School for over forty-four years, said she met Nancy and Marshall Benjamin through her children, who—along with many others—had to take buses out of town to attend school. Higginbotham noted that she and her husband moved to Florida from Birmingham, Alabama, because her husband was an engineer for Pratt & Whitney. "That was one of the reasons I think Marshall and Nancy built the school in this area," she said.

"There were so many engineers who were interested in a different kind of education—a private education—for their children." Joanna Hogan and her first husband were also drawn to the area by Pratt & Whitney. Their son required tutoring, which led them to the North Palm Beach Private School, where she befriended Nancy Benjamin. Mrs. Benjamin needed an assistant and asked Joanna, who took the job and continued teaching there for more than forty years. The Benjamins remained deeply involved in their local community outside of the school; Marshall Benjamin himself served on the planning board for the village.

Prior to starting the North Palm Beach Private School, the Benjamins were directors of the Belvedere Private School in West Palm Beach. They were both very experienced educators, as they also taught in Africa for the U.S. State Department for two years. Nancy Benjamin graduated from the University of Michigan, and Marshall Benjamin graduated from Wayne State University in Detroit. Nancy and Marshall Benjamin are remembered as kind and generous people who saw the need for a better education for children. When they decided to open their own school, they didn't expect it to become anything more than a kindergarten. As the demands for better schooling increased, the Benjamin School expanded, with additional space for students up to grade eight by 1993. The Upper School Campus in Palm Beach Gardens opened in 2004 to serve grades nine through twelve. The main campus is located in North Palm Beach, just off Ellison Wilson Road. "Mrs. Benjamin was a lot of fun," Margaret said. "In her later years, she always dressed to the hilt. One time, she said [to me], 'I didn't come here not to be noticed.'"

Marshall Benjamin believed that the students should be in a place where they could observe and enjoy nature, so instead of chopping down trees to build the school, the Benjamins chose to grow around the natural wonders of their new campus. This made for winding sidewalks, plenty of foliage and a special tree that has been on campus since the very beginning—inspiring students, parents and teachers alike. This tree also inspired the book *Treasures from Our Tree: A Collection of Remembrances from The Benjamin School Family, 1960–2003* by Trevor Romain. The Benjamins even did a lot of the manual labor around the school themselves. They dug and built paths, planted trees and made the school grounds beautiful.

In a little room inside the original school building, also known as the Benjamin House, Marshall Benjamin—Mr. B—gathered kindergarteners around him and taught them how to read. The wood floors and age of the little house seem to carry a certain kind of mystique. One of the child-sized chairs still sits against the wall inside this very room, which now serves as the headmaster's office. The original Benjamin House, sold to the Benjamins by the Rosses, was renovated in 1997 and moved to an area above the football field, where it is preserved and treasured as a part of the school's unique history and, subsequently, North Palm Beach's history.

Chapter 11

CREATING A LIBRARY, UNITING A COMMUNITY

To see [the North Palm Beach Public Library] *doing so very well makes me very proud and happy. You always have a place in my heart.*
—Nancy Moore, first official director of the North Palm Beach Public Library

The Library Society

When Ralph and Elizabeth Huls moved to North Palm Beach, they'd heard it was a good place for young families. But according to her daughter, Lisa, Elizabeth was taken aback when she arrived and realized that the village had no public library of its own—as were a number of other concerned citizens. Families with small children frequented the Society of the Four Arts Library in Palm Beach and the Mandel Library in West Palm Beach, but the commute to both of these locations was a long haul, especially considering that all of the borrowed books had to be returned within a week.

The idea for a local library in North Palm Beach originated within the local chapter of the American Association of University Women (AAUW). Thelma Obert was one of the founders of the local branch in 1959, and she was a major force behind the creation of the North Palm Beach Public Library. The library study committee formed a group of citizens, who approached the council to request money from the recreation budget. It took two years of hard work to make any real progress toward building a library.

Elizabeth Huls served as the first president of the Library Society, and she worked alongside Dr. Donald Bicknell, who helped lend his prestige and reputation to the project. According to one early member of the society, the founding of the library fell on the shoulders of the women, despite Dr. Bicknell's assistance. However, the North Palm Beach Lions Club was also instrumental in moving the project along. The club's support of the library project may have helped to finally persuade the village council that it was a good idea.

Lisa Huls Humbert remembered how much it bothered her mother that neighboring towns, including Lake Park and Riviera Beach, had their own libraries but North Palm Beach did not. As Elizabeth Huls became more deeply involved in the library effort, the Huls household transformed into a central collection point for book donations. Lisa was just two years old when her family moved to North Palm Beach, and she said that her earliest memories revolved around the library and its beginnings in her home. "We had shelves of books in the living room, and my mother had one of those woodworking irons—librarians used them—and you put white material on the spine and wrote on it with a hot iron." This tool was used to imprint the books' Dewey Decimal numbers on their spines.

The Library Society later used a room in the fire station to store its collected books while it looked for a permanent location.

> *My mom spent a lot of time there. Then* [the books] *went to the country club,* [the old Winter Club], *and I helped. I was five or six. They let me shelve books. That's always been my second home. Then, I remember when the plans were being drawn up for the current library. They were on my dining room table, and my mom would look at them. She was on the phone with people about it.*

Another member of the society recalled:

> *At that time, when we were accessioning the books, the books had to be shellacked. That's not done anymore. That was quite a process, because that little room got quite full…of the vapors and so forth. It was hot, so when we opened the door—there was no air conditioning in there—anyway, it was a very sticky situation all the way around because of the weather and having to do that. I remember the smell of the shellac to this day.*

When the Library Society began working toward forming an official library in the village, it faced some minor opposition. The village council was concerned about the cost. However, it eventually became clear that the community needed its own library. Despite being concerned about the budget, the council gave the group permission to move forward.

Fundraising and the Masquerade Frolic

In July 1963, the Library Society hosted an open house at their first location in the Winter Club. The Library Society's members, including Nina and Axel Kogstrom and Dr. Bicknell, who served as the society's vice-president, all participated in the event. The society announced that it was hosting a masquerade frolic for fundraising on October 26, 1963, at Captain Alex's

Some of the Library Society's early members were photographed on the stone steps of the Winter Club, the library's first official location. *Pictured from left to right, back row*: Warren Tatoul, Larue Dahlberg, Lorraine Hamacher, Helen Schick and Sally Boetel. *Front row*: Axel and Nina Kogstrom. *Nina Kogstrom. Village of North Palm Beach.*

Restaurant. Prizes were offered, including a grand prize of a weekend in Bimini for the best-costumed couple. Tickets were priced at six dollars per couple, and all of the proceeds went to the library to fund operations and purchase books.

In 1964, the library opened on the first floor of the old Winter Club. "There were big, wide stone steps and big doors," Lisa said. "None of the shelves were any higher than four feet, so you could see into the courtyard behind the castle. We called it a castle. It was mainly that big room there that I remember. It was beautiful there, with wood floors and big windows. I spent a lot of time there."

A CONTINUED TRADITION OF VOLUNTEERING

The library's collection of books and the formation of the library had previously been handled by the Library Society, but in 1965, the library was turned over to the Village of North Palm Beach. The village council library board helped manage the library and aid in its future growth. At the time, the members of the board were Kate Gildan, Seymour Bellak, Howard Campbell, James Gill and Martin Gold. Herb Gildan, the attorney for the village, personally dedicated a lot of time to the library project.

Despite handing over the administrative duties of the library, the Library Society remained active. While the library thrived on serving the village's close-knit community, individuals who lived outside the village could also get a library card for one dollar per year. In 1965, librarian Pauline M. Fancher wrote a poem dedicated to all the volunteers who helped build and nurture the library. These volunteers included Adelle Demers, Blanchie Pierce, Nina Kogstrom, Eleanor Nissen, Pamela Fitzgerald, Lee Emond and LaRoyce Campbell.

Helen Amendola offered to type up cards for the card catalog, so she took them home and diligently completed the task. A few schoolchildren also volunteered to help, and Pauline named them in her poem: Kevin, Marcia and Carol. Several people volunteered to run story hour on Saturday mornings, and they included Helen, Mrs. Reid, Paula Emond and Ed Jacomo, the director of the art center. Other volunteers at the library included Charlotte Patton and Margaret Schweizer. Pauline finished her poem with, "I want to thank you all for making what seemed an insurmountable task become small."

The Library in a Picturesque and Historic Setting

Nancy Fant Moore became the library's first official director. Nancy started out as a volunteer in 1962, when the library was housed in the Winter Club. She recalled how the circulation desk was located in the old barroom with a mirror behind it. Shelves were brought over on the back of a truck, while volunteers brought in donated books and painted a sign.

Nancy was a member of the North Palm Beach Library Society and the Woman's Club. Both groups were active in forming the library. Some people claimed the library was in the men's locker room of the Winter Club, while others said that it was located in the ladies' locker room. Nancy recalled that Thelma Obert referred to it as "the men's bathroom," but it was actually housed in the old dining room.

Betsy, who was the head of circulation at one time, volunteered in the library at the Winter Club. Nancy Fant Moore said:

> *We turned* [the women's locker room] *into a reference room, so the children could come and study in the afternoon.* [Betsy] *was the one who cleaned that room out. We had been using it as a storage space for papers. The Library Society came and put new drapes in and rugs on the floor and new furniture. It was a beautiful room. There's a picture somewhere of my oldest son and Pat Atwater's children in that room.*

In order to become an official library, longer hours were required. The village manager offered Nancy more responsibility, putting her in charge of evening hours. At first, she was impressed, but later on, she discovered no one else had been willing to work at night in the Winter Club. "They couldn't get anyone else because no one else was about to work in that old building at night. They said it was haunted," she added. Children who grew up in North Palm Beach believed Sir Harry Oakes had died in the Winter Club. "They would sit around the fireplace and tell stories about Sir Harry Oakes burning in that fireplace," Nancy added. Despite the legend of the haunting, she agreed to work on Thursday nights until closing. "I thought it might be one way to get out of preparing dinner for a husband and kids," she joked. "It was the [old] country club. I had the pleasure and honor of going there when it was the country club, and we had many good parties in that room. I remember it as the dining room and the library."

Nancy said she never loved a job as much as she loved her job at the old Winter Club. Although she began her work as a volunteer, she eventually became a paid employee. She felt uncertain whether she even wanted the job, so the village manager assured her that she could quit if she didn't enjoy it. Her first paycheck came in 1967. She had many duties, including mopping the floors when children would run inside after swimming in the country club pool, dripping water all over the floor.

CATALOGING WITHOUT COMPUTERS

In the early days of the library—before the use of computers—the process of acquiring and cataloging books was very different. The one constant, however, has been the Dewey Decimal System, which is still used today. The system of the card catalog simply switched to a computerized database. Nancy Fant Moore said:

> *We typed out our cards, put them in the backs of the books, and on page twenty-three, we stamped "North Palm Beach Public Library." It was very simple. Cataloging books today is a dream compared to what we used to have to do. We had to write everything down. For a long time, we would get the books and the card came with them, but we found that was pretty expensive, so we made our own cards. We had volunteers. We didn't have a computer.*

North Palm Beach Public Library acquired most of its books through donations, but when it came time to purchase a book, the library would look to a bookstore in Northwood in West Palm Beach. "We would go there to buy books," Nancy said, adding that they'd select the books and bring them over. "For the first five years, we operated in this fashion."

THE LIBRARY ON ANCHORAGE DRIVE

The cost for constructing a new library building was a concern for the village council, but Mayor Tom Lewis defended it, stating that the library at the Winter Club was already "far beyond the national average" in terms of the quality, number of books and variety of reading material offered. North

Mayor Thomas Lewis and his wife standing beside the dedication plaque in the main lobby of the library. *Village of North Palm Beach.*

The library dedication in 1969 also included a marine corps honor guard salute during the national anthem. *Village of North Palm Beach.*

Palm Beach, as a community of professionals, needed more space for its library, and he projected that the community's usage of the library would only continue to increase.

At noon, on October 24, 1968, Mayor Tom Lewis presided over the library groundbreaking at Anchorage Drive. The village's librarians attended, as well as those who'd served as president of the North Palm Beach Library Society. Kate Gildan, the chairwoman of the North Palm Beach Library Board, also attended. Councilmen, including Herb Watt, Tom Bell and Dave Clark, were also present. The Riviera Beach Jaycees donated their time to move books, shelves and furniture into the new location. The building cost $200,000, which didn't include the cost of the books and other materials. The government supplied an additional $100,000, but there still wasn't enough money to finish the first floor along with the rest of the building. Until it could be completed, the library only operated on the second floor.

To help cover the cost of books and other materials, the Library Society sponsored various fundraising events. When she started working at the new building, Nancy said that the library's staff was comprised of her, two pages and a few volunteers. The dedication of the new building took place in 1969, with Mayor Lewis presiding over the event.

FAMOUS WRITERS VISIT NORTH PALM BEACH PUBLIC LIBRARY

After the library moved into its new building, Nancy was given the official title of reference librarian. She ordered books and planned library programs. One day, a couple came into the library and talked with a young woman who worked at the front desk. She later approached Nancy and said, "This lady says her name is Mrs. James Michener. Do you think it's the real one?" Nancy walked into the stacks and pulled one of James Michener's books off the shelf. She opened the back of the book, looked at Michener's photograph and compared it to the man in the library. Sure enough, it was really him. Michener and his wife lived in Juno Beach at the time.

James Michener, the author of *Hawaii* and *Tales of the South Pacific*, became a good friend of the library, according to Nancy. He once complimented the reference collection, adding that he always found exactly what he needed whenever he visited. "He was the most down-to-earth human being," Nancy said. "He was quite admired." He once gave a book talk for aspiring young writers on the first floor of the library, and around two hundred people showed up. Mayor Al Moore, Nancy's husband, wrote to Michener in a letter dated April 8, 1982, to thank him. In the typewritten letter, Mayor Moore wrote "Dear Mr. Michener," but crossed it out and wrote "Jim," instead.

> *Just a brief note to tell you how much I enjoyed your program for our young, aspiring writers last Monday evening at the North Palm Beach Library. I can't remember ever seeing so many guests in our meeting room for any occasion in the past.*
>
> *I want to personally thank you for taking time from your busy schedule to speak to our writers and to answer their questions. You certainly made them aware of what it takes to become an author.*
>
> *There are too few men of your caliber who give of themselves to help others and have the community interest that you do. I sincerely appreciate it and extend my best wishes to you for your continued success.*
>
> *Sincerely,*
> *Al Moore*
> *Mayor*

Michener wrote a short piece on North Palm Beach history, which is now a part of the village's archives. Elmore Leonard was also a regular visitor to the library. According to Nancy, he lived at Old Port Cove and came into the library often.

Nancy Moore Officially Appointed Library Director

In 1984, Nancy was officially appointed library director. The village manager initially offered her the job when she was still a reference librarian, but she turned him down. Sometime later, he asked her again—this time telling Nancy that she'd only have to take the job for a little while until he found someone else. "I lasted twenty-two years," she said. She added that she'd later asked the village manager if he'd ever found anyone who might replace her, and he admitted that he'd never looked.

She retired in February 2005. The card catalogs were still there when she left, despite the fact that computers were being used. In an interview,

Nancy named other women who may have been interim or unofficial library directors before her—including Sharon Leiter—but the village's historical archives always point to Nancy as the first official director.

A librarian will often recall many amusing vignettes that they have witnessed through the years, and Nancy was no exception. "I should have kept a diary," she said. She described one funny incident that happened behind the circulation desk one day:

> *We had a new girl at the desk. She was a younger person and not really experienced in libraries. She had a phone call one day, and I heard her say, "Just a minute." She walked away and was gone for a little while, and when she came back, she said, "Not by that name. We don't have anything."*
>
> *When she hung up, I said, "Well, what did they want?" She said, "They were looking for someone by the name of Thomas Register." I had to turn and walk away, and then I burst into laughter. I said, "Honey, that's a set of books* [The Thomas Register of American Manufacturers]. *I'll show you where they are."*
>
> *She thought it was a man's name.*

Directors and Librarians Through the Years

When Nancy retired, Kathie Olds took over as the library director. Kathie had already been with the library as a reference librarian for about a year. The library has a short history of dedicated directors and some interim directors, including Donna Riegel, who was the director from August 14, 2006, to April 30, 2010; and Betty Lou Sammis, who was the director from July 5, 2010, to April 15, 2016. The library's reference librarians have included, of course, Nancy Moore, Karen White, Kathie Olds, Ann Burton, Betty Sammis and, finally, Diana Kirby. After working in the reference department for many years, Jeanne Saunders resigned in 2016, just after her ninety-first birthday. Some other notable staff members include Elvie Wright, administrative assistant, and Mary "Betsy" Taylor, circulation supervisor.

The Children's Department

Over the years, the library's group of dedicated children's librarians have included Marsha Warfield (1970s), Nancy Palmer (1990s) and Doris Pierce, who worked part-time. Susan Holmes joined the library staff in 1999; she started out in the children's department, where she managed two story hours. Susan later moved to the cataloging department, where she served as technical services manager until retiring in 2019. Mary Ann Caruso ran a story hour for toddlers. Nancy Hodges worked in the children's department and retired in 2013. She was followed by Dawn Hahn, who retired in 2019.

The Florida Collection

For many years, the Florida book collection was a centerpiece of the library, and it was housed in a back room on the second floor. Nancy Moore recalled how the collection grew slowly at first, simply because there weren't many Florida history books at the time. The Library Society alone donated thirty-five books to the Florida collection. "As soon as I would hear of [a Florida history book], we would certainly get it," Nancy said. Promoting Florida's history in the library became an important factor in increasing the collection.

"The village became occupied by people who were very well-known and prominent in the history of Florida," she added, noting the Atwater family. Pat Atwater was among the young women who banded together to form the Library Society, along with the Kogstroms, Elizabeth Huls and Thelma Obert. Over the years, Pat remained active in the library and was a part of the Friends of the Library until she passed away on December 4, 2017. She was ninety-two years old and the mother of Florida senator Jeff Atwater. "Pat Atwater made sure we got everything we were supposed to have, and bless her heart, I'm glad she did. The Florida room is absolutely beautiful," Nancy said. "I love that room. I'd like to take every one of those books home with me and read them all."

Thelma Obert Honored for Her Contributions

In October 1989, the village collaborated with the AAUW to dedicate the downstairs meeting room in the library to Thelma, renaming it the Thelma Obert Meeting Room. Library director Nancy Moore and Mayor Tom Valente took part in the dedication ceremony. In 1999, the Village of North Palm Beach gave Thelma the title of "Member Emeritus of the Library Advisory Board" for her dedication to the library as one of its original founders.

At the time, Nancy told the *Palm Beach Post* about Thelma's contribution. "Obert and a group of about twenty-five locals decided the town should have a library and investigated the need and financial requirements of starting one. Two years later, the group formed the North Palm Beach Library Society with Mrs. J. Edwin [Thelma] Obert as president." The Obert Room in the library remains as a permanent nod to the perseverance of a woman whom the *Post* called a "pioneer" in the founding of the North Palm Beach Public Library in 1989.

An Enduring Sense of Community

When Nancy Moore retired in 2005, she said she hoped the library would continue to retain its municipal status and not become a part of the larger county system. Nancy, who was born on November 30, 1928, passed away at home on June 19, 2014. She had worked with the library for forty-two years. The North Palm Beach Public Library continues to operate as an independent municipal library, with the same enduring sense of community that Nancy treasured.

Chapter 12

ART, CULTURE AND THE WINTER CLUB

They decided to have a fine arts program at the castle, so I took ballet there from Ann Strasnicsak. Her sister, Miss Jean, also taught, but Miss Ann ran the program.
—Lisa Huls Humbert, early resident of North Palm Beach

"Picasso Slept Here"

The Winter Club once stood near the present-day country club, which presides over the golf course. Someone wrote in the cement path that led to the mansion, "Picasso slept here." While some residents say this is true, others can't remember for certain. It has also been said that the Kennedy family had dinner at the country club restaurant in the early 1960s. Whether they are true or not, these legends add to the charm of the Winter Club—the building many remembered as "the castle."

When the library opened in the old Winter Club, Edward M. Jacomo had already been directing the municipal art center housed in the same location for three years. Jacomo earned his doctorate in New York and studied art at Penland School in Tennessee. He was born on May 23, 1942, in Maryland. After seeing a need in the village, he approached the council and told them that the town needed an art training program for its residents—essentially inventing his own position. The council agreed to give him a chance. Jacomo, who was well-liked, very young, friendly

This aerial view shows the Winter Club in 1957. The building wasn't available to serve as the art center until the second country club building was constructed beside it. *Village of North Palm Beach.*

and charismatic, was a discerning artist who questioned art theories and invented his own techniques and approaches to art instruction.

In 1960, the art center opened in the same building that housed the first firehouse. Six years later, Jacomo told the *Palm Beach Post* that the art center only had some newspaper and a couple of crayons when it first opened. When the new country club building was constructed in 1962, space in the old Oakes mansion became available. The Art Center moved there and quickly became a self-supporting hub of creative expression.

THE CULTURAL CENTER AT THE WINTER CLUB

Each year, the art center offered classes for two sixteen-week semesters, and in the summer, around 150 students attended art classes. The center attracted students from other towns as well. At its height, between 200 and

300 students were enrolled in classes that covered a wide range of subjects, including pottery, painting, interior design and crafts. The art center sometimes hosted unusual programming. Jacomo once told the *Palm Beach Post*, "And then there was the tiger—that surprised some people. It was a promotion for a brand of gasoline, and I persuaded them to bring the tiger here for a class. And, really, how many adults here would ever have a chance to sketch a live tiger? It was such a wonderful opportunity for them."

In 1966, the center offered twelve classes on a number of art forms, including pottery, drawing, painting, crafts and children's art. A registration fee and fee for materials covered everything, but non-residents had to pay an extra five dollars to attend the center's classes. These small classes became very popular, and they filled up quickly; people often had to be turned away. According to Jacomo, 50 percent of his students were young adults, 25 percent were children and another 25 percent were retirees.

Everyone loved Ed. He was often the recipient of gifts from his students, who gave him things like cookies, pies and soups. His children's art classes would sometimes go on field trips, which included trips to the beach to create paper-mâché crafts. They once went all the way to Cape Kennedy to learn about science for an art project. At the art center, imagination turned children's classes into more than just a structured period of time to create.

Jacomo encouraged the kids to play make-believe, which meant, if they were talking about outer space, everyone became astronauts and envisioned themselves in space or on another planet. This same sense of imagination was brought into the center's adult art classes. Jacomo would sometimes encourage his adult students to pretend that they were a particular public figure and to act in the way they pictured that person.

Jacomo—and the puppets he made himself—were the only employees of the art center. He single-handedly built a successful art enclave in the village by nurturing the artistic talents of North Palm Beach's residents. He put on puppet shows for the children, and he used his puppets as guest "teachers," who would instruct the kids in various subjects. Sometimes, he would also don a fun-looking hat—a Mexican sombrero or a French beret, depending on what part of the artistic world he was discussing. His students were children, engineers and housewives. He believed that anyone could be an artist as long as the thing they were creating meant something to them on a deep level of personal expression.

Transforming the Castle

The wine room in the mansion became a print-making studio, where old washing machine wringers were used as printing presses. Jacomo also used what had once been a meat pantry to store items such as clay and yarn. He encouraged his students to use anything and everything in their art projects by repurposing items from around the house.

Then-village manager Joseph Eassa Jr. was vocal about his support for the art department and for Jacomo's dedication and accomplishments. The *Palm Beach Post* quoted Jacomo: "A community owes more to its people than providing regular trash pickups. The goal of the art center has been to provide a stimulating atmosphere for creativity."

The North Palm Beaches Art Society is Born

In 1964, Ed Jacomo founded the non-profit corporation the North Palm Beaches Art Society. The society's members resided all over Palm Beach County. Jacomo himself often lectured at various art events around the area, and he served as a judge in local art contests. Members of the society were both professional artists and hobbyists. The organization offered its members opportunities for growth in their field, and in 1979, it began awarding scholarships to promising young artists who aspired to study art at a college or university.

The Ballet Department and the Cultural Center

By 1967, the art center at the castle had become such a large part of the community that Mayor Tom Lewis proposed an idea of creating a cultural center in North Palm Beach. The idea surfaced when the council discussed forming a ballet department. Ann Strasnicsak already taught ballet through a contractual agreement with the village, and her class, at that point, had grown to 120 students. In the art center, ballet classes were coordinated by the ballet office. It was also a big year for Ed Jacomo's art classes, which brought the largest number of registered students—186—into the classroom. Every month, the art center held art exhibitions with a variety of talented local artists.

According to a 1968 article in the *Palm Beach Post*, "The ballet center occupies the Old Country Club with the art center and the public library. It is part of the village's cultural program and is a non-profit educational and aesthetic institution owned and operated by the municipal government there." Because the art center's classes were growing, it was reasonable for the council to consider how to hire new teachers and categorize the classes.

Ann Strasnicsak (maiden name Mollica), who was born on March 2, 1907, was a popular teacher. She was also a member of the Business and Professional Women's Club of the North Palm Beaches and the Women's Civic Club of Riviera Beach. Lisa Huls Humbert, whose family lived in the village for nine years before becoming one of the first ten families to move to Jupiter Farms, remembered taking ballet classes with Miss Ann and art classes with Ed Jacomo.

> [Ann's] *sister, Miss Jean, also taught there, but Miss Ann ran the program. We had our ballet recitals out in the courtyard of the castle, out back, and they would build a stage and bring lights. My dad* [Ralph Huls] *ran the lights for a couple of years. I got to go into the back passageways—maybe they were servants' stairs—and go up in there and watch the proceedings from up top while the bigger girls were dancing.*

Ann Swiatowski, who grew up in the village, remembered her second communion breakfast at the old country club building. "I took ballet there and gymnastics," she said. "We were really little."

Jacomo Leaves a Legacy Behind Him

In June 1967, after eight years of running the Art Center, Jacomo accepted a teaching position at Alma College in Alma, Michigan. After inspiring so many people in North Palm Beach to follow their artistic dreams, Jacomo left Florida. The Winter Club would never be the same. The North Palm Beach Art Center became a staple of the community, and much of it was due to Jacomo's hard work. Besides being a place where residents learned artistic techniques, the Art Center also attracted professional artists. In the

Ed Jacomo resigned as director of the art center when he accepted a teaching position at Alma College in Alma, Michigan. *Pictured, the Alma College art faculty (1969–1970) from left to right*: Ed Jacomo, displaying the charismatic energy for which he was always remembered; Jeff Blatt; Jan Bowen; and Kent Kirby. *Alma College Library Archives.*

summer of 1969, several professional artists attended classes to experiment with new techniques, according to an article in the *Palm Beach Post* published that May.

ART CENTER ATTRACTS PROFESSIONAL ARTISTS

The new director of the art center, Norma Y. Rachlin, graduated from the Rhode Island School of Design. Her work has been shown in many galleries and exhibits, and she won awards at both the Norton Gallery in West Palm Beach and the South Florida Fair. Artist Joan Lustig's work appeared in numerous local galleries and museums, including the Norton Gallery and the Flagler Museum. In the summer of 1969, she joined other passionate creatives at the art center to experiment with etchings. Jayne Waterman, another award-winning artist, also attended classes. Waterman majored in art at Shimer College and went to the American Academy of Art in Chicago.

When artist Ed Valicka came to the art center, Norma was excited to welcome him, along with the others. His educational background included time at the Cleveland Art Institute and the Columbus College of Art and Design, and his career had taken him to many corners of the art world—from newspapers to art agencies and studios. His work in advertisement had appeared in nationally distributed publications.

Donna Tweedle won awards for her work at the art center, where she studied her craft. She also majored in painting at Wesleyan College. Through varied art classes, this cultural center of North Palm Beach offered more than just art classes to pass the time for hobbyists—it gave dedicated artists the chance to learn and teach new techniques and expand their horizons. The Winter Club was the center of all the activity in the village; it offered inspiration and knowledge by nurturing an art enclave in the northern Palm Beaches. The village owes its thanks to Ed Jacomo for walking into the village hall and proposing the creation of an art department.

Ed Jacomo Continues to Inspire

Throughout the remainder of his career, Jacomo continued to inspire his students and involved himself in projects that endeavored to challenge how people viewed artistic expression—remaining on the very same path he'd walked while he was an inspiring art educator in Florida. In 1974, the publication *Art Teacher* featured an article on a bus that Jacomo turned into a traveling gallery. He used the bus to bring exhibitions to local

Edward "Ed" Jacomo was a professor of art at Alma College from 1968 to 1980, when he left Florida. He passed away at the age of fifty-one in 1993. *Alma College Library Archives.*

schools in Michigan. In 1976, he was honored with an award from the Michigan Art Education Association for his contribution to art education. Meanwhile, the heartfelt and ambitious influence that Jacomo made on art education in the early days of the village helped shape the artistic expression of many local children and adults. Jacomo passed away in 1993, at the age of fifty-one.

Chapter 13

FROM ONE ERA TO THE NEXT

[North Palm Beach] *is truly a village that was well planned, and which turned out beautifully.*
—The 25th Anniversary of the Village of North Palm Beach: An Official History, *village historian Bill Young*

Always Growing

When the village was first incorporated, it was a small town that was still building a network of resources for residents. Mayor Darryl Aubrey, who spent a lot of time playing golf with his father-in-law, remembered both the Winter Club and the second incarnation of the country club, which opened in 1963.

> *There weren't a lot of houses then. They were building it pretty rapidly, but the village was nowhere near built out in the 1960s. My father-in-law* [passed away] *in the early 1960s, and that ended my* [earlier] *connection with the village.* [When my wife and I] *retired, we finally found a place in North Palm Beach. It's a great place to live.*

THE TWIN CITY MALL

In the interest of progress, a four-thousand-square-foot building was opened in July 1971 as the Twin City Mall, situated on Northlake Boulevard, on the border of North Palm Beach and Lake Park. The mall cost $10 million to build and featured a Sears, GC Murphy's and Orange Bowl eatery, among other businesses. Mayor H. Mallory Privett Jr. of North Palm Beach and Mayor Donald K. Jorden of Lake Park presided over the ribbon cutting.

The mall brought hundreds of jobs to the area, and Sears provided the most—about four hundred. Bill Turner, originally from Kentucky, joined the team as the mall's first manager. Events at the mall included art shows and sales sponsored by the North Palm Beaches Art Society.

The mall didn't last, however, and it took some time for the property to be re-zoned, as half of the mall was in North Palm Beach and the other half was in Lake Park. Around 1990, the last business vacated the mall. In 1991, a task force that represented both towns tried to invite Florida Atlantic University to use the building as a temporary north county campus, but this plan never came to fruition. In the late 1990s, the structure was demolished. As of this book's publication date, a Publix supermarket now resides on the lot along with other businesses.

EXPANDING THE VILLAGE

Before condominiums were built on U.S. Highway 1, in the northern part of town, the Ross brothers owned a part of the land. They had a plan to develop the land themselves, but they later sold it to Llwyd Ecclestone, who then built Old Port Cove. In 1970, Ecclestone's company, the Florida Realty Building Company, began work on this condominium complex, which, at the time, was projected to cost around $72 million. Advertisements billed Old Port Cove as a place that would offer a unique water-centered lifestyle for those who didn't necessarily want to own a house. The grand opening of the community featured a "water weekend," which started on Friday, October 23, 1970, and included outboard racing events with prizes and trophies. Advertisements referred to the event as the First Annual Old Port Cove Invitational Regatta.

Constructed on sixty acres of land, Old Port Cove comprised eight separate towers once it was completed. Before its construction was finished, Ecclestone projected that the apartments would cost between $25,000 and $50,000 each. Construction was not complete until 1982.

The Next Great Project

In prosperous times, development was thriving in North Palm Beach and South Florida, although it was sometimes difficult for real estate projects to find funding. Christine Schwencke recalled that Dick Ross was the more aggressive individual in the partnership between the Ross brothers, Jay H. White and her father, Jack Schwencke. "He was always looking for the next project," she said. She added that he would come into the office and announce that he thought they should purchase a piece of property. At one point, he wanted to buy the land where the Palm Beach Gardens Mall now stands. Back then, it was nothing but empty sand and brush.

Jack Schwencke was still involved in real estate in the 1970s, and in 1973 and 1974, he started two condominium projects—Gemini and Aquarius. The Gemini project was named for Christine and her sister, who were both born in June, and those condominiums were built on a piece of land that overlooked the Intracoastal Waterway in northern North Palm Beach. Aquarius Condominiums stood on Singer Island. However, when the Arab oil embargo went into effect, people stopped buying. Schwencke had planned to invite Jeane Dixon, a well-known astrologer, to the opening of the condominium complex, but this never came to fruition. John D. MacArthur later bought Aquarius and sold the units at cost.

The Herb Watt Building and the Shuffleboard Courts

In early aerial photographs of the land surrounding the Anchorage Drive library building, a small building, along with shuffleboard courts, can be seen beside the library. When this small building was constructed in the early 1960s, it was only used as a shed for the shuffleboard courts, but additional space was eventually needed for club activities and recreation. A meeting room and a kitchen were added on to the building, and it was named after Councilman Herb Watt, to honor his vocal support of senior citizens in the community.

The Herb Watt Building eventually proved to be too small. Many clubs had meetings there, including the North Palm Beach Yacht Club, a bridge club and the Garden Club, but in the late 1980s, it became clear that more space was necessary. The council began to discuss whether the building should be demolished or kept.

The Herb Watt building and shuffleboard courts once stood on the site of the veterans memorial next to the North Palm Beach Public library on Anchorage Drive. The North Palm Beach Yacht Club adopted the building (*shown in 1997*) as its regular clubhouse. *Joseph A. Tringali.*

The Village Hall faces U.S. Highway 1. In this aerial photograph from 1970, the Herb Watt building and shuffleboard courts are shown beside the North Palm Beach Public Library. *Village of North Palm Beach.*

Even though the village was young, some councilmembers felt it was a piece of the town's history and didn't want to see it go. The council considered moving it, but because it was built on a concrete slab and had additions, this wasn't a feasible option. The building had already closed once—in 1988—but it reopened when the yacht club decided to use it as a clubhouse. The village already had a community center and parks to offer its residents and clubs, so the Herb Watt building was eventually torn down, along with the shuffleboard courts.

Air Force Beach to MacArthur State Park

From the 1940s to 1956, black and white servicemen from the Palm Beach Air Force Base at Morrison Field—now Palm Beach International Airport—utilized the stretch of beach that would later become MacArthur Beach State Park because it had a private, non-segregated beach. The area was soon referred to as Air Force Beach. At the time, it was a remote area that was privately owned by John D. MacArthur. The two-mile space within the bounds of North Palm Beach later became known as a great place to go skinny-dipping.

According to rumors, MacArthur himself enjoyed swimming in the nude and didn't care what people did there. The spot had become a well-known nude beach by the late 1970s, but when the state purchased the property in 1982, it was decided that the beach would not be clothing-optional. In the early days of the village, young people often spent a lot of time at Air Force Beach, hanging out and having parties with friends. In 1989, the area became Palm Beach County's only state park, the John D. MacArthur Beach State Park. The park remains a jewel in North Palm Beach and encompasses Munyon Island as well.

MacArthur Beach State Park, 2012. *Author's collection.*

PROTECTING PEANUT ISLAND

The little manmade island in Lake Worth, next to Riviera Beach, was used for picnicking, fishing and recreation, but its future became uncertain in the late 1960s. North Palm Beach residents and those in the surrounding towns wanted to protect it as a recreation area. Members of the North Palm Beach Garden Club were among those who wrote letters protesting any other use of the land.

The Port of Palm Beach issued a ninety-nine-year lease to Peanut Island Properties Inc. (Ocean Development Corp.), which permitted them to build an oceanography center on the island. The development of the center would have included the construction of a bridge to the island, offices, research labs and aquariums and a public park with a one-thousand-foot-long beach. Those who were against the proposition were concerned that the development wouldn't stop there. They were worried that developers might try to build high-rise condominiums on the island as well. Although developers denied this, there were still whispers about potential apartment buildings, a hotel and more.

Save Peanut Island Inc. was formed on April 13, 1970, to try to reclaim the island and protect it as public property. In December 1970, Mayor Tom Lewis voiced his support, requesting that Peanut Island be preserved "to give youth what is rightfully theirs—a stable environment in which they can rear their children." All of the surrounding towns also had something to say about the proposed development. The main concern of Save Peanut Island Inc. was that developing the island would damage the ecological balance of the area. In August 1976, Peanut Island was rezoned as a "preservation-conservation" area by Palm Beach County commissioners, who decided that the island should remain an unspoiled recreation area. Today, Peanut Island Park is managed by Palm Beach County Parks and Recreation Department.

Chapter 14

THE WINTER CLUB CONTROVERSY

The mansion at 951 U.S. Highway 1 has been ruled unsafe by the Village Building Department. It has deteriorated greatly with age and with weathering. Externally, huge trees almost cover the older part. The windows are mostly boarded up…

—*"History of the North Palm Beach Country Club,"* The Murder of Sir Harry Oakes: North Palm Beach Folklore, *Marilyn Robson*

Years of Neglect

The Winter Club remained a fixture in the village. It was the center of community activity and a point of reference for residents and visitors who never forgot "the castle" in North Palm Beach. Its cultural center provided many hours of enjoyment and learning for both children and adults. However, very little was done to care for the structure, and certain parts of the building were eventually marked as off-limits.

The iconic mansion remained in use even after the new country club was opened, but residents recalled that it wasn't taken care of as well as it should have been. The controversy over how to handle the situation began in the late 1970s, as the village council started to deliberate. In 1979, a referendum regarding the fate of the Winter Club that went before the

The back patio of the Winter Club when it served as the North Palm Beach Country Club, 1957. *Village of North Palm Beach.*

council resulted in a tie—1,103 voted in favor of restoration, while 1,103 voted in favor of demolition.

The first floor of the Winter Club was still being used for dance classes and as an office space. In the 1960s, the basement had been used for art, dance and gymnastics, but in the late 1970s, it was empty and deemed unsafe to enter. The upper stories were also boarded off to keep people out. No one could agree on what to do with the club, and the argument droned on, even as the mansion remained in use.

DEDICATED GROUP SEEKS TO PROTECT THE WINTER CLUB

Residents who wanted to save the mansion began to band together to protect it. Village manager Raymond J. Howland, historian Martha Nadleman and library director Nancy Moore were among those who were trying to get the building recognized as a historical site. Marilyn Robson, who wrote about the history of the mansion for a college paper, said, "Every one of my informants, after telling me the tales associated with the club, expressed complete opposition to the idea of destroying the mansion. I do agree. Do not destroy our village history."

The original nomination to add the Winter Club to the National Register of Historic Places—which was received on June 5, 1980, and accepted on August 1, 1980—called the condition of the building "deteriorated." Years of neglect had built up, despite the club's continual use as a cultural center for art, dance and office spaces, and soon, the repairs became too expensive to undertake. Still, many residents felt that the building was worth saving. Built by Harry Kelsey and Paris Singer in 1926, the Winter Club eventually became the center of village life, and to many, it was the heart of the town. Marilyn Robson recorded her memories of the mansion from when she was a child: "When I was ten or twelve years old, we used to take art lessons in the summer....We used to climb up in the old tower....The windows were all broken out. You could hear the eerie cooing of the birds, and you could always hear the trees rustling."

As Nancy Moore and others focused on protecting the mansion and contacting local media about their efforts, they tried to keep the legend of Harry Oakes out of the discussion. They wanted to share the history of Harry Kelsey and how he came to build the Winter Club, rather than focus on Oakes's involvement as a one-time landowner. Nevertheless, Moore noted in an interview with Marilyn Robson that the local news sources still brought the Oakes murder into their reporting of the preservation efforts—probably in an effort to add a bit of "spice" to their reports.

Nomination for the Registry of Historic Places

The nomination to add the building to the National Register of Historic Places was reviewed, approved and entered on August 1, 1980, by the National Parks Service in Tallahassee. The building was marked as a historic place and added to the registry—but the battle to protect it was far from over.

It appeared that the last structural upgrades that were added to the building were completed in 1935, when Harry Oakes still owned the estate. According to the original nomination paperwork, the mansion had a large interior space that could serve as both a ballroom and a dining room. It went on to state, "This area has been partitioned, creating two smaller rooms used for both arts and crafts classes and ballet instruction. This main section also had a half basement which ran the

The Winter Club. *Village of North Palm Beach.*

length of central block. The basement served for storage and had lockers for persons using the facility."

In 1983, as talk about the Winter Club's fate continued, lawyer Theodore Babbitt formed Save the Winter Club Inc., with the goal of preserving the Winter Club as a historical part of the village. However, due to the fact that the local municipal government had not done enough work to keep the building in good repair, Babbitt's efforts were futile.

Richard Cavanah knew Ted Babbitt—they were neighbors. "I thought the Winter Club should have been saved," Richard said. "After they put locks on it, I had a key, and I would take my senior swimmers in there to work out with weights. It was a great big room with terrazzo floors. The recreation department had balance beams for gymnastics [in there]. I don't think it should have been torn down." Until recently, he'd kept a wooden beam he salvaged from the old building when it was demolished. The solid construction was evident. "The nails were still as good as new," he added.

SAVE THE WINTER CLUB, INC.

According to the Florida Department of State Business Registration, Save the Winter Club Inc. was a non-profit corporation formed on October 11, 1983. Along with Babbitt, the company had four principals listed on the record: Jeri Athey, Nancy Moore, Jane Smith and Margaret Turney—all residents of North Palm Beach.

Nancy Moore was involved from the beginning and helped get the nomination process started. Richard remembered the group well. "They went to Tallahassee to get the building recognized as a historical place, and it should have been," he said. He added that Margaret Turney was a realtor. Save the Winter Club Inc. was made up of "the old guard of the village," and they tried everything they could to save the building, including proposing ideas for building and renting office space around the Winter Club to help fund repairs and continued maintenance on the building. "The committee estimated it would take $1 million to renovate and then $100,000 a year to keep it going."

The paperwork for the National Register of Historic Places described the south tower's living quarters, which included a kitchen, bedrooms and bathrooms.

> *The 1935 Oakes addition provided the owner's quarters with a large living room, complete with a terra cotta ornamented fireplace. The clubhouse's interior walls are plaster, and* [there are] *acoustical tile panel ceilings in many rooms* [that] *conceal the original wood ceilings. Bedroom flooring is wood, while terrazzo is found in the central block. Much of the original ornamentation has either been removed, covered or painted over.*
>
> *The clubhouse once boasted a patio-garden area behind the west (rear) side of the building. The once expansive grounds have been consumed by the construction of a recreation complex and Olympic-size pool. Presently, due to code violations, much of the building is unused and has suffered from exposure, deterioration and inadequate maintenance.*

The nomination further described the building's red barrel tile roof and stucco walls, as well as its irregularities, which included towers flanking the large central part of the building. "The north tower functioned as a kitchen, servants' quarters and shower and locker facility for the club's guests," while the larger area in the center was the dining hall and ballroom. "The south tower provided sleeping quarters for the owner, with separate kitchen facilities and bathrooms. The 1935 addition acted as a large living room, accessible from the south tower of the clubhouse." Richard noted that, in 1982—close to when the building was finally torn down—"they put a new barrel tile roof on it for [about] $43,000."

Temporary Restraining Order Helps Buy Time

The building's relevance in the area's history qualified it as a historic place. The report noted how the building's connections to Kelsey and Singer also made it important to the development of Lake Park and Palm Beach County overall. It also noted the Winter Club's architectural significance and its legendary connection to Harry Oakes. The mansion was truly a landmark that painted a rich image of Palm Beach County's beginnings.

For a while, it seemed as if Babbitt and Save the Winter Club Inc. was going to succeed. They managed to stave off the destruction of the club, and even after a demolition crew accepted a bid for the job, they persuaded the court to hold off for ten days. Palm Beach circuit judge Lewis Kapner issued a temporary restraining order in October 1983, which allowed Save the Winter Club Inc. to prepare for a hearing.

An ordinance that was meant to protect the Winter Club drew scrutiny from the village council, which wanted control over what happened in and around the building. Save the Winter Club Inc. backed the ordinance, which required the village to preserve the building and allow an outside entity—or residents—to restore it. This meant that a private business, such as a restaurant, could operate within the Winter Club and help raise the funds necessary for preservation. However, the council at the time felt that it wouldn't be wise to allow a private business in competition with other local businesses to operate within a town structure.

Demolition on the Horizon

Despite being involved in the initial efforts to protect the Winter Club, village manager Ray Howland was soon on the other side of the controversy. For many, including Howland, it appeared that even if the building was protected, the cost of repairs would be too great for the village to absorb. On August 8, 1984, Howland met with Delta Demolition Inc.—the company that had been given the bid to raze the building—and learned the cost of demolition would be $17,143. Meanwhile, Marilyn Robson noted in her report that repairs to the structure would cost as much as $300,000. Howland told the *Palm Beach Post* that he expected protestors to show up on the first day of demolition. Babbitt told the same news reporter that he hoped residents would hold an "organized farewell" to the Winter Club.

Although Babbitt and Save the Winter Club Inc. worked hard to collect signatures for petitions and battle in court, things didn't work out as they had planned. The building would've been demolished on November 1, 1984, if not for the restraining order, but when the March 13 referendum ballot went out, the club's future was sealed; 1,525 residents voted to save the building and 1,692 voted to raze it. A mere 165 people turned the tide against Babbitt's fight to save the mansion. "We got the public to vote, but it was against us. It was an empty victory," Babbitt told the *Post*. Save the Winter Club, Inc. had become a thorn in the town council's side. North Palm Beach obtained estimates for the demolition of the Winter Club, but because of the setbacks caused by Babbitt's persistence, town officials requested that Save the Winter Club Inc. pay over $3,700 to settle the difference between the new estimates and the initial demolition bids.

The Winter Club was torn down in 1984, and the move remains a controversial one. Richard Cavanah remembered being in the pool, teaching his swimming students, when demolition began. Everyone stopped what they were doing and watched the last remnants of a bygone area fall, broken, to the ground.

The fight to preserve the Winter Club was lost in 1984, when it was torn down, despite having been added to the National Register of Historic Places in 1981. *Richard Cavanah.*

> *The building would have lasted if they hadn't voted to tear it down. They had a pottery kiln downstairs. On the second floor, they had art classes, sewing and bridge. One big room used to be the country club dining room before they finished* [the new building] *in 1963.* [The Winter Club] *was the library at one time. It had terrazzo floors. The recreation department had an office in there when I first came here.*

The building didn't have any termites, Richard said, but it did have honeybees. "On the main floor, on the back side, in the wall, you could feel it was really warm. It went five feet into the wall and was probably full of honey," he added. "One little hole in the stucco and you could see bees coming and going." Richard said the two banyan trees on the property have likely been there since the Winter Club was first built. These trees, and the last small set of steps from the original building, are all that's left of the Winter Club.

A number of the village's residents felt that the building should have been preserved, but the last vote finalized its fate. Lisa Huls said it was a town landmark. "North Palm Beach was like a bedroom community, but if you said, 'It's where the castle was,' everyone knew what you were talking

The demolition of the historic Palm Beach Winter Club, 1984. *Richard Cavanah.*

The last surviving remnants of the Winter Club are these stone steps. In this photograph, they are surrounded by construction while the new country club is being built, June 2019. The Winter Club once stood to the right of these steps. As of this writing, they are still there. *Author's collection.*

about. I spent so many hours climbing in those [banyan] trees," she added. "We were there all the time, either with my parents or riding our bikes over." The Huls family resided on Pelican Way when Lisa was a child. The children rode their bicycles to Lighthouse Drive, over the bridge and around to Anchorage Drive until they reached vacant land. There, they would cross the empty land and ride to the golf course. Over many, many trips, the children wore a path in the sand and brush. "It was a different time," Lisa said. "For us, it was a long ride."

After the town lost the Winter Club and the art center, the North Palm Beaches Art Society found a gallery home at the Crystal Tree Plaza on U.S. Highway 1. In 1988, twenty-two years after Ed Jacomo founded the society, it reached its initial goal of having a permanent gallery in Northern Palm Beach County. Next door to the Art Society Gallery, there was a small art school that was run by the society. It offered classes in various techniques taught by professional artists. In the early 1990s, the society held meetings at the North Palm Beach Public Library and had gallery showings around Palm Beach County. There is no evidence of the original society's longevity beyond 1992.

While the parks and recreation department has offered many activities and classes for both adults and children over the years, nothing has ever come close to the inspiring and energetic environment that Ed Jacomo created and nurtured at the North Palm Beach Art Center in the Winter Club.

Chapter 15

LOOKING TOWARD THE FUTURE

I have a Ross [brothers] *home. I'm living in the same house. We added on rooms as we had children. We moved here in 1957. When we moved in, there wasn't anything built north of Flotilla Road.*
—Claire Hill, North Palm Beach resident

MOVING FORWARD

Jack Schwencke retired and played in bridge tournaments in places like France, Paris and Morocco. He became a nationally famous bridge player, and when he traveled the world, his daughter Christine said that he would tell everyone he was one of the original developers of the Village of North Palm Beach.

Bob Ross eventually moved to Miami before he relocated to New York City. His brother, Dick, bolstered by their great successes in Florida, tried to replicate the successful model behind the development of North Palm Beach in Vermont. For some reason, however, the Vermont project didn't have the same level of success as the Ross brothers' endeavors in Palm Beach County.

From Mayor to Congressman

Tom Lewis, who served the village as mayor from 1965 to 1970, went on to become a congressman and represented Florida's sixteenth district in the House of Representatives. He passed away at the age of seventy-eight in 2003, and he is remembered as a "straight-shooter" who "nobody ever had a bad thing to say about." His contribution to the formative years of the village helped shape its future.

Public Safety Building Named for John S. Atwater

When John S. Atwater retired from the FBI in 1978, he took on the job of public safety director in North Palm Beach, and he served in this position for about ten years. Overall, he was involved in the department for about twenty years.

The Atwater family became an important part of North Palm Beach's continued history. John's wife, Pat, remained active with the Friends of the Library of North Palm Beach, and his son Jeff became a Florida state senator. In 2006, the village named the public safety building on U.S. Highway 1 after John Atwater. Then-public safety director Jimmy Knight—who would later become village manager—led the ceremony. The event's speakers included Mayor David Norris and John's son J. Michael Atwater.

Historian Resolution Continues to Work for the Village

Although the village was young, its early founders and officials recognized the importance of preserving North Palm Beach's history. On August 24, 1978, the village council passed and adopted a resolution to create the volunteer position of village historian. On January 12, 1979, a letter from Palm Beach County regarding federal historic preservation funding was addressed to "Ms. Martha Nadleman, village historian." Martha was the first historian appointed by the village council under the 1978 resolution.

Over the years, the council has continued to appoint village historians, who work to record and preserve the village's history. William "Bill" Young, who was born on October 2, 1909, lived in the village for forty-three years

The 25th Anniversary of the Village of North Palm Beach: An Official History by Bill Young. *Village of North Palm Beach.*

and was one of the town's first elected councilmen. He served as the village historian from 1981 to 1990, and he wrote the first official history of the village, which was published in booklet format for the twenty-fifth anniversary of the founding of North Palm Beach.

Charlotte Young Doten, Bill Young's daughter, recalled that her father was very proud of North Palm Beach. Bill grew up in New York City, where his father was a judge. His little sister, Elizabeth Young, went on to become a movie star, who was best known for her role in the 1933 film *Queen Christina*. Bill chose to become a realtor, and he attended Cornell but never graduated. He moved his family from Vermont to North Palm Beach in 1957, drawn to Florida by a job in real estate. Charlotte said of her father:

> *He was very patriotic. When World War II broke out, he was in his thirties. He enlisted. He'd gone to New York Military Academy. He was discharged* [as a] *lieutenant colonel. He was very well read, enjoyed history and politics. He wanted to make a difference. He cared a lot about the*

Bill Young when he was in the army in the early 1940s. *Charlotte Young Doten.*

Bill Young and his wife, Mary, 1960s. *Charlotte Young Doten.*

> *village. He was one of the very first elected councilmen. Those before him were appointed. He felt very strongly about North Palm Beach...and was very proud to be* [village historian]. *He was partly retired by then and spent a lot of time on the booklet he wrote. He considered that* [official history] *to be, probably, his greatest accomplishment. He saw nothing but good things for the village.*

After Bill Young, more dedicated individuals stepped forward to serve as the village historian and help raise the awareness of North Palm Beach's history: Vivian Brichta, James Gentemann, Norv Roggen, Dolores Walker, Eugene Bryan and Carol Wood.

In 2003, Dr. Joan Aubrey was appointed to the position and served until 2011. Dr. Aubrey was responsible for acquiring materials and creating a gallery of village history that was displayed for about eight years in the Obert Room in the library. The display was set up as part of the fiftieth anniversary commemoration, and it was presented in conjunction with a recorded history that walked viewers through each historic photograph. In honor of the fiftieth anniversary, village resident Charlotte Chickering also compiled a history of the village, which was published in booklet format as a follow-up to Bill Young's written history.

For many years, the library on Anchorage Drive has housed the town's archives and the village historian's office. In 2010, the author of this book, Rosa Sophia Godshall-Holden, was appointed village historian and served until 2014. She was followed by Lynn Holden, who resigned from the position in 2016. Thanks to the council's resolution to maintain a village historian, North Palm Beach's history has been recorded for future generations. Much of the archive is now available online via the village's website.

Time Capsule Preserves Village History

During the celebration of the twenty-fifth anniversary of the founding of North Palm Beach, a time capsule made by Pratt & Whitney was filled with mementos and buried in front of the library. Those who visit the library today can find the plaque that marks the burial spot in front of the outdoor book drops. "Mrs. Margaret Turney was in charge of that operation and in charge of the capsule," recalled Nancy Moore. "Lots of the information [about the village] went down [in the capsule] when we celebrated the twenty-fifth. It was mainly village resident information, and children from the school sent over things, like pictures of how things were at that time," she added.

The capsule was pulled up again as part of the fiftieth anniversary annual Heritage Day celebration, and Nancy was, once again, present for this event. At the fiftieth anniversary celebration, she served on the committee for the event and was in charge of the capsule. Judy Pierman, a councilmember who had already served as the village's first female mayor after being elected in 1989, was also on the committee for the event. Nancy said, "We pulled up [the capsule], took it into the meeting room and had tables set up. We placed [the items] on the tables." Many of the people who'd donated items at the twenty-fifth anniversary celebration were present for the fiftieth, including Bill Young's adult children. At first, Nancy said, the lid on the capsule wouldn't come off. "One of the Pratt & Whitney engineers said, 'Just hit a hammer to it.' My husband, who was a Pratt & Whitney engineer, used to say that [too]," she said, laughing. "They hit it with a hammer, and sure enough, it popped off."

Photographs of the area that had been placed in the time capsule showed how much things had changed. "They took a picture of how U.S. 1 looked in 2006 [and put it in the capsule]," Nancy said. "You wouldn't believe what happened in that period of time just on U.S. Highway 1." Sports memorabilia from the capsule included golf balls that had been donated by Jack Nicklaus. "We tried to get different things from different people in the sports world—things that will be of interest twenty-five years later," Nancy said when she was interviewed in 2011. "All the former mayors came. We had all kinds of activities." The time capsule is slated to be reopened in 2030.

Veterans Memorial Park

William Manuel, who was originally from Massachusetts, moved to the village in the early 2000s and became active in local politics. His focus as mayor was the Veterans Memorial Park next to the library, which had just been a landscaped lawn area after the Herb Watt building and old shuffleboard courts were removed. The idea for the Veterans Memorial Park was conceived in 2009. To pay for the park, the village decided to use money it had already set aside for recreation and town beautification, rather than use any taxpayer funding. Construction began on July 22, 2013.

The brick walkway around the park doubled as a memorial for those who wished to purchase a brick engraved with the name of a loved one. The path wound through the small park, which offered benches, trees and a trellis filled with vegetation. Six flagpoles with emblems from each branch of the military and commemorative plaques completed the memorial park. The park was Bill Manuel's biggest accomplishment as mayor. He passed away on February 21, 2015, and his memorial service was held at the park.

Jack Nicklaus Signature Golf Course

The North Palm Beach Golf Course and Country Club has gone through many changes over the years. In 2005, the village enlisted the help of professional golfer Jack Nicklaus to redesign the golf course for a fee of only one dollar. In late 2006, the course reopened as a Jack Nicklaus Signature Course. It is one of only two such municipal courses in the United States.

The construction of the Veterans Memorial Park began in 2013. The park was built on the former site of the Herb Watt building and the shuffleboard courts. *Author's collection.*

The course continues to be a popular destination for golfers in Florida, and it is listed on the Florida Historic Golf Trail through the Florida Department of State. The course was also listed in forty-ninth place on the list "Top 100 Golf Courses." In 2017, the North Palm Beach Country Club building—which was dedicated in 1963—was demolished to pave the way for a brand-new club building, which was completed in 2019.

FESTIVALS AND FAMILY FUN

In 1987, the village began hosting its very own arts and crafts festival. Early festivals were co-sponsored by the North County Junior Woman's Club. When Joseph A. Tringali served as mayor, he suggested that the town should create a family-friendly annual event called Heritage Day. In May 2000, the first Heritage Day festival and parade took place, with

During the annual Heritage Day Parade, awards were given to the most creatively decorated float. The library float (*pictured*) was the winner on several occasions. *Shown from left to right:* Maddie Drake, Fiorenza DelGuzzi, Shayn Neary and Francesca DelGuzzi. *Betty Lou Horne Sammis.*

plenty of fun for both children and adults at the country club. The fiftieth anniversary celebration of the village's founding, complete with a 5K run, took place as a part of the Heritage Festival in April 2006.

Each year, the village's departments and advisory boards build floats for the parade. Often, prizes are given. A regular winner in the past was the library's float, which focused on a creative literary theme. The village also holds an annual tree-lighting ceremony during the holidays. The parks and recreation department, which offers programs within the village, also runs "Trips and Tours," which include day trips to destinations like the Miami Book Fair, the Elliot Museum in Stuart and many more. The village continues to offer a sense of community and fun to its residents and maintains the adage that it is "the best place to live under the sun."

Going back to try for the "big one" that got away yesterday

Every development we inspected lacked one or more of the elements we considered necessary to insure our future happiness and investment. Finally we discovered the village of North Palm Beach; it appealed to us immediately. Here was an entirely new, perfectly planned community, situated on miles of waterfront — the perfect spot for a couple of fishing enthusiasts! While fishing is our hobby, our decision to live here was based on the many major advantages the village had to offer. We were impressed by the new village hall, the modern water and sewage disposal plants, and the plans for the new school to be built this year. Landscaped streets and sidewalks were in and paid for. Police, fire and sanitation departments were in full operation. Gas, electric and telephone services are available to every lot. The future of our investment is assured through strict zoning regulations. Another very important feature is the North Palm Beach Country Club — it's the center of social activities for the village; and another added incentive for living in the village of North Palm Beach!

One of our favorite fishing spots only minutes away from home

you get MORE for your money in

This 1956 advertisement highlighted the reasons that North Palm Beach was an attractive place to live. Mr. Paul Thomason and his wife, both longtime residents, are featured in the advertisement. *Village of North Palm Beach.*

Today in North Palm Beach

The police and fire departments eventually grew and separated. The current public safety building on U.S. Highway 1 was constructed in 1999. The activities and classes that once took place at the old art center in the Winter Club—now a distant memory—continue in some fashion through the parks and recreation department.

In 2014, the North Palm Beach Elementary School building—the first public school in the village—was demolished to make way for the newly created Conservatory School at North Palm Beach, a charter school that offers a concentration in music and performing arts for children. The music program is the school's main focus. Another private school option was offered to local families when Baldwin Prep School opened on the south side of the village in 2003.

In 2019, a new country club building was completed, and the country club pool received major renovations. Despite continued changes throughout the village, the Village of North Palm Beach maintains the community atmosphere that the Ross brothers, Jack Schwencke and Jay H. White aimed for when they made their careful plans and carried out development in 1955 and 1956. By looking back to the past, we can see where we've come from—and where we're headed.

BIBLIOGRAPHY

Aiello, K. *The Benjamin School: 50-Year Anniversary, 1960–2010*. North Palm Beach, FL: Benjamin School, 2016.

Andrews, E., and C. Andrews, eds. *Jonathan Dickinson's Journal, or God's Protecting Providence*. Hobe Sound: Florida Classics Library, 1985.

Bickel, S. Personal interview. February 18, 2018.

Chickering, C. *The 50th Anniversary of the Village of North Palm Beach.* North Palm Beach, FL: Village of North Palm Beach, 2005.

Corbett, Daniel Kribbs. *History of Juno Beach*. Juno Beach, FL: Town of Juno Beach, 1992.

Florida Department of State. "Florida Historic Golf Trail." www.floridahistoricgolftrail.com.

Gateway: The Magazine of the Port of Palm Beach. "Munyon Island: Yesterday and Today." May/June 1993, 8–14.

Gooding, Dorothy Borden. *Tucked Between the Pages of Time: A History of Lake Park and Environs*. N.p.: Self-published, 1990.

Higginbotham, J. Personal interview. April 2019.

Higgins, S. Personal interview. December 12, 2018.

Historical Data Systems, comp. "U.S. Civil War Soldier Records and Profiles, 1861–1865." Provo, UT: Ancestry.com Operations Inc., 2009.

Historical Society of Palm Beach County Archives. Available at the Richard and Pat Johnson Palm Beach County History Museum in West Palm Beach, Florida.

Hogan, J. Personal interview. May 2, 2019.

Knott, James R. "Sunday Brown Wrapper" articles. *Palm Beach Post.*

Kriplen, Nancy. *The Eccentric Billionaire.* New York: AMACOM, 2008.

Lake Park Historical Society Collection. Available at the Lake Park Historical Society in Lake Park, Florida.

Lynch, J. "The P&WA Connection." *United Technologies: Bee-Hive*, Summer 1978, 17–21.

Palm Beach Post, archived articles.

Paraizo, L. Personal interview. May 7, 2019.

Robson, Margaret. Personal interview. December 12, 2018.

Robson, Marilyn. *The Murder of Sir Harry Oakes: North Palm Beach Folklore.* Unpublished manuscript, 1979.

Romain, T. *Treasures from Our Tree: A Collection of Remembrances from the Benjamin School Family, 1960–2003.* North Palm Beach, FL: Benjamin School, 2003.

St. Clare Catholic Church. www.stclarechurch.net.

Young, W. *The 25th Anniversary of the Village of North Palm Beach: An Official History.* North Palm Beach, FL: Village of North Palm Beach, 1981.

ABOUT THE AUTHOR

Rosa Sophia currently serves on the board of the Seminole Wars Foundation. She also volunteers with the Loxahatchee Battlefield Preservationists as the organization's archivist. From December 9, 2010, to March 27, 2014, Rosa served the Village of North Palm Beach as its official historian, maintaining and digitizing the town's archives with the focus of making the history of the village easily accessible to residents and researchers. A portion of her essay on the history of the North Palm Beach Public Library, based on earlier research, was published in the book *Overdue in Paradise: The Library History of Palm Beach County* by Palmango Press in 2017. This book won a silver medal for Florida nonfiction in 2018 from the Florida Authors and Publishers Association (FAPA). She is also the author of several novels, including *Meet Me in the Garden* (Limitless Publishing, 2015). She has worked as a library specialist for North Palm Beach Public Library, and the Martin County Library System, and she is a member of the Society of Florida Archivists. Rosa lives in Palm Bay, Florida, where she is a writer and managing editor for *Mobile Electronics magazine*, the nation's number one resource for the 12-volt aftermarket car audio industry. She is pursuing an MFA in creative writing at Florida International University in Miami.

www.backwordswriter.com